TRUTH OF A HOPI

Stories Relating to the Origin, Myths and Clan Histories of the Hopi

TRUTH OF A HOPI

Stories Relating to the Origin, Myths and Clan Histories of the Hopi
Edmund Nequatewa

A & D Publishing
PO Box 3005
Radford VA 24143-3005
www.wilderpublications.com

ISBN 10: 1-60459-033-5
ISBN 13: 978-1-60459-033-3

First Edition

This is one of the rarest types of ethnographic documents, one actually written by a native American. Mr. Nequatewa ably relates some of the mythological stories also covered by Voth. However, the bulk of this book—by far the most valuable section—covers the historical legends of the Hopi, from a Hopi viewpoint. The Hopi 'theory' (Nequatewa's word) was that the 'Bahana' (the white people) emerged from the under-world alongside the Hopi, and went off in search of the truth. Someday they would return and live in harmony with the Hopi, bringing wisdom and great abundance.

So what is the truth of a Hopi? The return of the Bahana didn't work out quite that way. The Hopi resisted enculturation, sometimes through armed resistance, at other times through nonviolent resistance (as when they hide the children from the policeman coming to take them to the boarding schools). However, all the while they apparently kept their good natured belief that someday their ironic 'theory' of the inherent goodness of the whites would work out.

Throughout, Nequatewa relates incidents and characterizations of Hopis that go far beyond the 'Noble Savage' sterotypes of brave warriors and laconic wisemen. The Hopi who occupy these pages are all too human, and that alone is a drop of truth that is missing from accounts of the Hopi, even to the present day. —J.B. Hare

Table of Contents

FOREWORD

The stories related in this little book represent the origin, myths and history of a group of Hopi clans. They carry us from the very beginning of things down to modern times. One might say that they are the "Old Testament" of these people. They tell of their origin, their sacred beliefs, their wanderings and their trials. The first story is one recounted only by the Priests of the "One Horned Fraternity" in the village of Shung-opovi. Edmund Nequatewa, a Shung-opovi man who recorded this story, is of the Sun Forehead Clan and is a member of the One Horned Fraternity. Clan stories are not supposed to be told by the members of unrelated clans but members of the powerful One Horned Fraternity may tell all the clan stories belonging to the clans of their village. Each society has its own group of stories and sacred songs which it may give, but no other society is supposed to know these or to relate them.

The clans concerned in this particular story are the following: the Bear Clan, *Hona-wungwa*; the Strap Clan, *Bia-quois-wungwa*; the Blue Bird Clan, *Chosh-wungwa*; the Spider Clan, *Koking-wungwa*; the Gopher Clan (extinct), *Mui-wungwa*; and the "Greasy Eye Cavities of the Skull Clan," *Wikurs-wungwa* (now extinct). Other clan stories are included in this book.

The Crow, *Ungwish-wungwa*, or Kachina Clan story is closely connected with the first story, the "Truth of a Hopi," and their later history forms a part of our tale. These people came to the Hopi towns after the arrival of the Strap Clan and the Parrot Clan, Gash-wungwa (Zuni Clan from Awatovi).

The Legend of Palotquopi is the story of the Cloud or Water Clan group; these were the last to arrive. Several of these clans are mentioned in our main story. The Cloud, *Omow-wungwa*, or Water Clan (nicknamed Flood Clan) was originally the Corn Clan, *Ka-eu-wungwa*. After the disaster at Palotquopi this clan split and three others were formed, the Snow Clan, *Nuva-wungwa*, the Wilted Corn Clan, *Pikas-wungwa*, and the Rabbit Bush Clan, *Sivaf-wungwa* (now extinct). With these clans came the Eagle Clan, *Qua-wungwa*, the Tobacco Clan, *Bif-wungwa*, the Rabbit Clan, *Taf-wungwa*, the Sand Clan, *Teu-wungwa*, the Bamboo or Reed Clan, *Wuko-bacab-wungwa*, the Sun Forehead Clan, *Kala-wungwa*, originally the Eagle Clan, and the Sun Clan, *Tawa-wungwa*. When this group arrived, the Crow Clan was already settled at Mishongnovi by the Corn Rock.

The clans mentioned above, with which the three stories deal, represent all the clans in the village of Shung-opovi, with the exception of the following group: Badger Clan, *Honan-wungwa*, Butterfly Clan, *Poval-wungwa*, Tansy Mustard Clan, *As-wungwa*, and the Parrot Clan, *Gash-wungwa*, said to be a Zuni Clan. These clans came from Awatovi, after the destruction of that village.

As the North American Indian never developed a written language, all traditions are passed down by "word of mouth." Boys were initiated into the sacred societies when they reached early maturity, and were then taught the traditions and history of their people. Since the intrusion of the White Man and the development of his school system, there has been a consequent breaking down of the ancient customs. Although the young men are still initiated into the societies, it is usually at a much later period and often even after marriage. The old men complain of the careless inattention of the younger generation and are fearful that their history and traditions may fall into confusion and be forever lost to the coming generations. And so, today we find many of the more thoughtful men anxious to have these precious records permanently recorded in writing.

In the following pages the author's style remains practically unchanged, only slight alterations having been made here and there by the editor for the sake of clarifying the meaning. Historic events have been checked by the editor and many explanatory foot-notes added.

The author and the editor are greatly indebted to Dr. Harold S. Colton, Miss Katharine Bartlett, Mr. Lyndon Hargrave, and various Hopi informants for their kind cooperation and assistance in compiling this little book.

MARY-RUSSELL F. COLTON, *Editor.*
Flagstaff, Arizona,
September 1, 1936

CHAPTER I

HOW THE PEOPLE CAME OUT OF THE UNDERWORLD

ALAIKSAI!—Attention. Before anybody's memory the Hopi lived in the underworld, which was the original place of all human life. Here, in the beginning, all life and everything was good in peace and happy. The people were governed by the chiefs (*Mongwi*), village criers (*Chakmongwi*), priests (*Momwit*), and high priests and all their religious rites were ruled by the high priests. The people were classed as common, middle, and first class.

The time came when the common and middle class of people grew wise to the doings of the priests and the high priests. All the days of their lives these poor people had been cheated of their family rights by the upper classes of the people. At times the wives of the lower class were visited by these men and by the priests and high priests, while the poor husbands of the women were away. Now all this kept on from bad to worse.

By this time the wives of the priests and the higher class of men also grew wise to what had been going on for all these years, and they were greatly troubled. Then, gossip, quarreling and fighting started between the men and women. Some priests said that it was a joy to cheat and steal another man's wife and that they would pray hard and earnest for prosperity. The women in return said, "If this is so and true, would it be more joyful to you men if we did the same to you as you have done to us? Would you then pray harder still for prosperity?"

This question was, of course, asked by decent women brought up before guilty men and at this, every heart was troubled. The women turned their husbands away. They had no place to go but to their gathering places, called kivas, which were the underground houses—meeting places at times of ceremonies. In these kivas some hearts were sad and some did not seem to care so very much. They were all waiting and watching to see who would leave the kiva first to go to their houses to see if their wives would refuse to let them in. Some women had declared that they would not let their husbands in, so they put their belongings outside of their doors.

The men left the kiva one by one, going to their homes to try their wives, but finding their things outside, they had to go to the homes of their relatives. Even there, they were not welcomed and were not invited to cat, so they were forced to take two or three ears of corn to the kiva to roast. That was all they had for their meal on that day. The night came on. What were they going to do? This was the question. Some said they would stay in the kivas and live on roasted corn as long as they could, thinking that the women might get over this trouble and their anger.

While the wives were still feeling strong against their men, they called a council. Every woman was present. At this council it was decided that the men would be falsely forgiven and would be taken back by every wife. All this was followed out and the husbands were made happy. But knowing all this, the chief, Yai-hiwa, and village crier, and their families, were greatly troubled and were sad. A thought came to the chief's mind of what he should do and how he must punish his people. Now with all this he was troubled in mind. About this time, when the men had been falsely forgiven, the women were going around and running wild after the unmarried boys, so that they might break the hearts of their husbands and so be revenged. Their families were neglected and their fires and cookings were left unattended. Among both men and women there was not a soul who could be happy in such sinful days, for there was murder, suicide, and every other wicked thing that made the days darker and darker.

All this worry and sorrow was on the chief. What could be done? Nobody knew. So he went calling on his wise men (*Posi-wiwaimkum*) personally, and broken hearted as he was, he could not help but shed tears at every call. These wise men were named Kotiwa, Tani, Sootiwa, Komay, Seytiwa, Nawiki, and Kowisa, and they were the best of all wise men, with high ideals. But everything was for the chief to say in those days, so he asked every wise man to come to his counsel on the fourth day, out at a distant place away from the people.

The day came and the chief was out early that morning. With his bag of tobacco and pipes he was waiting for his wise men to come to the appointed place. One by one they came, each with his bag of tobacco and his pipe. The village crier was the last to arrive, and now everyone had come who was expected. Here they kindled a fire and being weary and sad they were rather quiet, sitting around their fire. The chief filled up his pipe with tobacco, lit it and smoked, then passed it to Yai-owa, the village crier. He puffed the smoke four times, then looked up to the chief, saying, "Father." In return the chief said, "My son." The pipe was passed on around in the same manner to every man. After the chief's pipe was all smoked out, every man filled his own pipe. Every pipe was first handed to the chief. Here they had their fatherly and brotherly smoke.

When the smoking was done the chief said, "My dear fellowmen, I pray in hopes that the gods, our fathers, get the smell of our smoking that they may have mercy upon us. With their power, I pray we will succeed and win because of what I have planned to do. My dear fellowmen, it is this. We must find a new place somewhere and we must find some way to get out of this sinful land, either below or above. I am in hopes to save some of you people if you only could realize this and feel as grieved as I do, about the trouble we are having this very day. I pray you to help me." Everybody was silent, arms folded, heads down over their knees while the chief was speaking. Every word was heard.

Then they said, "Our father, our chief, we pray with all our hearts and we are ready to help you. We will stand with you. We will walk in your path and whatever you ask of us we will do."

"Very well," he said, "be watchful and look ahead in my path that I may not mislead you. I pray you all and hope that the words you have spoken are from the very hearts of you and are true."

"We pray you, chief, that the words we speak are from every heart, and they are true."

"Very well, my fellowmen, I thank you. We will get busy at once. Tomorrow we will make *pahos* (prayer offerings) for our gods asking for the mercy and blessings that they bring upon us. I, the chief, Yai-hiwa, again thank you all. Be here earlier tomorrow."

The men went to their homes with the hope of success in their hearts, for they were true, honest men and were loyal to their chief.

The next morning being the second day of the meeting, the chief and all his wise men came to the same place where they had met the day before and here they smoked, as usual. Every man had brought his material with which to make pahos, or prayer sticks.

"Now," said the chief, "my dear fellowmen, let us start our work, and let every heart be in earnest. Let no soul be discouraged for we must work till we succeed."

"Our father and chief, we are strong in heart to be with you. There is no thought in us to forsake you."

"Very well, I thank you all," said the chief.

So here they made their prayer sticks all the forenoon and part of the afternoon. The chief had done his cutting of the pahos first, then the rest had copied after his, for he knew every sort of cut for a certain god. All this was well done."

When they had finished their paho making, every man, with his tray or plaque full of prayer sticks held in front of him, again circled around the fire and filled his pipe with tobacco to smoke. With a Hopi, smoking a pipe is the most true and earnest way of showing himself in prayer. Here they let the smoke pass from their mouths onto the trays of their prayer offerings to let the gods know they were earnest. With the Hopi, the smell of the smoke is the most sincere message to the gods, and for this reason much smoking is done at the times of all ceremonies. Now the work was well done for that day, so the chief said, "This will be all for today, and tomorrow we will see again what we can do. Let us all leave our pahos here and four of you will stay to guard our things, while the rest of us will go home and get something to eat. Then we will all come back and will bring you something to eat, and from now on we will camp here to the finish."

This was the third day of their session. The four men stayed to watch, so that nothing would harm their prayer offerings, for they afraid that the witches and the wizards might send a spy to find out what was going on, for it has always been believed by the Hopi that the witches and wizards could change their form into anything—into wild animals or birds of any kind. The men who had gone home all came back and brought food for the rest that had stayed. Now they were to take turns that night in watching, so that nothing could come close enough to see what kind of pahos they had made. They did this and at last morning came and the watchmen had done well.

Then the chief called his men to come together and take their places in a circle, and their smoking started, asking for mercy and the blessings of the gods, and all this was done. And again the chief looked up and said, "My dear fellowmen, our work is done so far, but we must have someone—we must call somebody who is wiser than we are to do the rest, or to finish the work for us. So let us now sing the calling song." With this song they called the mocking bird, *Yapa*. Now when he came he asked them, "Why do you want me? What can I do for you?"

The chief said, "We are in great need of you for you are so much wiser than us all, and you know all the songs of our gods. We need your help. We want to be sure that we make no mistakes. This is why we have called for you to come, and so we did make some pahos for you."

The chief handed him a tray of pahos, and the mocking bird was very glad to receive the prayer offerings. This was the fourth day when the mocking bird was called.

After receiving the prayer sticks the mocking bird said, "Yes, I am called a wise bird and one that knows everything, and of the songs I know all. But there is still somebody higher than I and he is above me, and this one is the canary bird, *Si-katsi*. Make no mistakes, call him. If he comes and says for me to help you, then I will, for he is still the wisest of all and his advice we must follow. Now I must go and hide for I do not want him to know and grow jealous because I came first."

The mocking bird left and was gone. Then again they sang their calling song for the canary bird and he came and sat on a nearby bush.

"Welcome," said the men, and he flew and sat down right in the center of them.

"Why do you call me?" he asked. "Why do you want me here?"

"Yes," said the chief, "we called you because we are in trouble and you being the wisest of all, we need your help. With all my heart, truly and honestly I pray you to help us."

"You are right," said the bird, "I am always in all prayer offerings. My feathers are always first. The trouble you are having I know all about. I wondered why you have waited so long to call me."

"My dear bird," said the chief, "it is like this. Our minds are full; we are almost insane and cannot think right, so do not think we mean to pass you by."

"I understand you," said the bird, "so I am here to help you. But I cannot do everything alone. I cannot perform my ceremony without the magic songs. The mocking bird must be with us. Call him at once. We need him."

Again the Hopis sang their calling song and soon the mocking bird was in sight. As he came near everybody said, "Welcome."

"Yes, here I am," said the bird, "Why do you want me?"

"It is I," said the canary. "Without you and your magic songs nothing could be done."

"Certainly, being noted for my songs I feel that it is my duty to be here and help you," said the mocking bird.

Before getting things ready for the ceremony, the two birds flew back around the rocks and there they changed their form into human beings. When they came back, the Hopis saw that they were handsome tall men with long straight black hair.

Now all this time the men were getting the things ready with which the Birdmen were to work and perform their ceremony. In laying the altar they spread out the sand in a small square and in the center they placed a sacred water bowl and for each direction an ear of corn was placed. Each ear of corn was of a different color-yellow for the north, blue for the west, red for the south, and white for the east.

When the altar was set up, they were ready for the mocking bird to take the lead in singing. The first songs were for making up the medicine water in the sacred water bowl. After the medicine water was :made, the calling songs were to be next, but the questions arose: who would they call first? Who would have the courage and strength to go out to find a place for these Hopis to go, where they might rest and live in peace? The two Birdmen knowing all things, the Hopis left everything to them that there might be no more trouble. So they first called the eagle, *Kwa-hu*. At the end of every song the sacred water was sprinkled to each direction.

As they were singing the eagle came and sat in the midst of them and said, "Why do you call me? Why do you want me?"

"Welcome," said the men. "You being strong on the wing that is why we call you. We want you to help us. We think that you might find a place for us that we may be saved, and we pray that you will."

"Even though being a bird of the air and strong on the wing it is a hard undertaking. But with all my heart I am willing to help you, so let us hope for the best and pray our gods that I may come back to you alive. To be sure, which way must I go?" asked the eagle.

"We wish you would go up into the skies. There may be an opening and another world up there," said the men.

When the eagle was ready to fly and the prayer feathers were tied around his neck and upon each foot, the eagle said, "Pray that I may find a place up there and bring good news." Then off he went up into the skies. He circled round and round above these men and they watched him as he went up, till he was no more to be seen. At last it was getting late in the day and the people felt rather uneasy about him, but finally he was seen coming down, and now it was very late. It seemed as though he was just dropping down, and sure enough he was. He was hardly alive when he came and dropped in front of them all, exhausted, and they rushed to him and rubbed him till he came to. Soon he was quite well and had come to himself again. Then he was ready to tell the news.

"I know you are anxious to hear how far I have gone and what I have seen. Well, my dear good men," he said, "to tell you the truth, the way up there is rather discouraging. When I left here and kept going higher and higher, not a living thing was to be seen above the clouds. As I went on going higher I began to wonder where I would rest, but there was nothing to light on and nowhere to get a rest. When I looked up, it seems as though there is an opening up there, but I was getting very tired already, and if I didn't start to come back I might not be able to return here alive and tell you this news."

After hearing all this they were very much troubled and deep in sadness,, and they wondered what else must be done. The eagle then received his prize of many prayer offerings and was asked to stay with them to the finish, and, of course, he was glad to be with them.

By this time the two leaders—canary and mocking bird—thought of someone else to call. Again they were singing the calling song, and in singing the song it was mentioned who they wanted. Before the fourth song was half sung, a hawk, *Ki-sa* came and circled above once and sat down in the midst of them and said, "Why do you call me? Why do you want me?"

"We call you because we are in trouble and we need your help," said the men.

"Yes, I do know that you are in trouble," said the hawk. "All who have a heart wish to help and save you, and I am willing to do whatever you will ask of me."

"Very well," said the Hopis, "we want you to search the skies for us . You are strong on the wing and can fly high, so we feel that you might be able to find a way out of this wicked world."

"Very well," said he, "I will try."

So they made ready for the hawk to fly and put prayer feathers on him as was done to the eagle—around his neck and on his feet.

When he was all ready, he said, "Pray with all your hearts that I may find a place for you and bring you good news."

"We will," said the men, "for we want to save our families and many others who have good hearts, so may our gods take care of you while you are on the journey."

Up the hawk went and circled round and round overhead, as the eagle had done. For a long time he could be seen up in the air till he was gone above the clouds. All this time the men were singing prayer and luck songs that nothing would happen to the hawk.

It was getting late and everybody was rather uneasy again, and they kept watching for him very anxiously. Finally, he was seen again, but he did not seem to be alive and the eagle did not wait to be asked but went right up to meet him. Then every heart was troubled because they thought that he was surely dead. Now, before the eagle knew, the hawk had dropped past him, and then he just dived for the hawk, to catch him, and when the eagle did catch him his mouth was wide open but his heart was still beating a little. When the eagle came down with him in his claws he laid him down on a white robe and every eye was full of tears. Soon one of the men started to rub him, while the mocking bird sang the "life returning song." When he came to he was quite weak, and earnest prayers were shown by smoking many pipes for the hawk. Now by this time he was ready to tell his story.

"I know," said the hawk, "you are all anxious to hear what I have found out for you up in the skies. When I left here, the first part about going up is the same as what brother eagle had seen and told you. I had gone as far as he did, then I took the courage upon myself and went on up as far as I could see up there. I am quite sure that there is an opening up there, but I was tired out and was not able to go any further before I knew that I was dropping down. I tried to turn myself over, but could not make it, for I was exhausted. Finally I felt something hurting me on my sides. I opened my eyes and found myself in the sharp claws of brother eagle. Then, I do not know how we got here, but now I thank the gods and you all that I am alive again. But let us not be discouraged, we might find someone that will make it up there and find out for us all about what is up there. I know every heart is in trouble. My heart is in trouble too because of you."

After hearing this story of the hawk, there was very little light in the hearts of the men. But the thoughts with the men were still very deep of what is to be done next, or who would be the third to try the skies for these Hopis. Everything and everybody was very still and quiet—prayers were being said by the smoking of many pipes.

The next morning being the fifth day of their ceremony, the wise Birdmen—canary and mocking bird—called the men to attention, to come around the altar and fill up their pipes by which to say their prayers again to the gods. After this was said and done, they started singing the calling ceremony again, but they did not know who they were calling this time. Before long something came and just went "whip," sounding like a whip over their heads many times and then sat down in the midst of them, and he was a swallow, *Powvowkiaya*.

He said, "Here I am."

"Welcome," said the men.

"Why do you call me? Why do you want me?" said the bird.

"Yes," said they, "we need you. We want you to help us out of the troubles we are having. We want to be saved."

"I know you do," said the swallow. "I was anxious and longed to be called, but I know your minds are full and of course I know the way things have happened, so I have no envy against those who were called first, because I may not be able to equal what they have already done, but do understand that I am willing to help you."

"Yes," they said, "you being strong and swift on the wing, we pray in hopes that you will make it up through the skies to find a place for us, and here we have these prayer feathers made for you to wear on the way."

"Thank you," said he, "I would be happy to have them, but all those might be in the way so I will go without them."

"Very well," said the Hopis, "you know best of how you go in the air. May our gods bless us and have mercy upon us so that nothing will happen to you and we pray that our gods may take care of you on your journey and bring you back safely to us, so pray that no heart may be discouraged."

"You have all said well. I thank you all," said he.

Then he went off and in a little while he was out of sight. The men filled their pipes and were smoking. Those who were not smoking were singing the prayer songs of good luck. Again it was getting late in the day and the men were still strong with smoking and singing, while the eagle and the hawk were looking up into the skies with their sharp eyes. Finally they saw that the swallow was coming and they hesitated not, but flew right up to meet him. When they reached him he was nearly done and with a faint voice he said, "Catch me." They made a dive for him and did catch him and brought him down and right away they gave him some water and started to rub him up till he had come to himself. While he was resting the gift of prayer feathers was given to him.

When the chief handed all this to him, he said, "This is our gift to you, from us all. We are glad that you have returned to us again."

"Yes," said the swallow bird, "and I know you would like to hear what I have seen and done. It is too high up there. What these two brothers and I have seen is too great and wonderful, and to anybody without wings it is dangerous because the wind is strong up there. Going into the opening I got scared of the wind and was afraid to go any higher for fear I may not be able to come back. If I did I might not be alive to tell you this. What all I did see I could not begin to tell you all about it."

Now the Hopis were wondering who would be the next one to fly into the skies for them, so rather hopelessly they filled their pipes again to smoke and to pray some more, and of course they were very silent.

Finally the canary bird spoke up and said, "My dear fellowmen, we will make our last try so we will call brother shrike, *Si-katsi* and see what he can do for us. He is pretty wise too, so cheerfully come to the altar and we will sing again."

They all moved up around the altar and took up a little more courage, hoping down in their hearts for success. Before many calling songs were ended someone came flying very close to the ground and sat down on top of a nearby bush and from there into the midst of them.

"Welcome," said the Hopis.

"Yes, yes, here I am," he said. "Why do you want me in such a hurry?"

"Yes," said the mocking bird. "Here we are in trouble. Brother canary and I have been working here with these Hopis trying and hoping to find a place and a way to save them from this sinful land. These three brothers here have done their best up in the skies and they all seem to be very certain about an opening somewhere up there. This is why we wanted and called you, hoping that you can find another world and save us."

"With all my heart," said the shrike, "I am here to help you. I know and feel that it must be a hard undertaking because these three brothers were not able to make it. But to be sure, you must all tell me if you are all earnest in the hope to be saved. Somebody's heart must be bad here and he is the one that is holding you back and keeping you working so hard. Every heart must be true and honest. Let us all be one if we really want to be saved."

The chief of course was most troubled to think of all that time he had spent and had not yet accomplished anything, for he, himself, had good faith in his men and trusted them. Anyway, he asked the people then if there is any one of them with a false heart and who is intending to forsake them and they declared themselves to their chief and father to be all true men.

"No fault having been found in you, it gives me courage to go on and take the trip," said the shrike, "so pray for the best while I am away." He went off on a slow flight and as he went higher, he kept going faster. Soon he was no more to be seen. The men then took their pipes, filled them up and smoked with all their hearts, while the canary and the mocking bird were singing their prayer songs. The eagle and hawk were keeping their sharp eyes looking up into the skies.

Praying for many days with their pipes, every tongue was burning with the taste of the tobacco, but their courage was still strong for they were hoping for good news with all their anxious hearts. The day seemed very long.

It was very late when the shrike was seen high up in the sky and he was very slowly coming down. The eagle and the hawk saw that he was still strong so they did not go up to meet him for his little wings were still holding him up. As he was coming down nearer everybody was asked to hold their heads down with high hopes that he may land safely. As he landed they felt that their prayers were answered and they were filled with much joy. The shrike was asked to be seated in the center of them and be resting while the men joined in prayer by smoking their pipes.

When this was done the chief said to the bird, "I am more than glad and happy to see you come back to us again and it is not only I, but everybody here who is anxious to hear the news of what you have for us, so let us hear you."

"It is the same story," said the shrike, "from here on up to where these others had gotten to. When I passed that, I could see the opening and from there on the passage looked rather narrow. As I went on higher into the narrow passage, in there I found many a projecting rock on which I could light and rest myself. Then, at last, up through the opening which is just like a kiva you have down here. The light and sunshine is much better than here, but there is no sign of human life, only the animals and birds of all kinds. Now the question is, how are we going to get you up there? Because even the strongest birds carrying you one by one could not get you all up through there."

"So it is," said the chief, "that is another hard proposition, but let no heart be discouraged. Let us all be strong and we will succeed and leave our troubles behind here in this sinful world for I am more than glad and happy to know that there is another and better world up above, so if there is anyone present to give us advice of what is to be done next, I would like to hear him."

"It is I, who am called Kochoilaftiyo (the poker boy) said a boy who was sitting way in the back. They did not even know that he was with them all this time, for he was ranked and considered as of the low class people.

"Come forward to my side," said the chief.

And he was seated on the left side of him. Being only a poor boy it was rather doubtful to the others that he would know of any advice to give, but he was treated like the others and so they smoked their pipes together. When this was done, the chief asked him of what he had in mind.

"It is not much of anything," said the boy. "But I am with you and with all my heart I wish to help you. You know and everybody knows that I am not recognized nor respected half as much as the others."

"You have spoken the truth, but you must forget that now," said the chief. "You who are with me here, I refuse no one."

"I thank you," said the boy with eyes full of tears. "I know a little creature, *kuna* (chipmunk), who lives on the nuts of the pines. I think he knows how to plant and grow those pines and he may have some seeds. If he would come and plant and grow us one of those tall trees it might reach the sky so that we may climb up on it. He lives in the rocks and pines."

"Very well," said the chief, "let us call him." At this he turned to the mocking bird and asked him to sing his calling song for the chipmunk. At the altar the mocking bird picked up his rattle and started to sing. It was not very long before the chipmunk appeared over the rocks with his usual chip-chip voice, and when he did come up he ran in front of the altar.

"Why do you call me, and why do you want me?" he asked.

"It is because we are in trouble. We need your help."

"I am ready," he said.

"As you are noted for your tree planting and know how to make them grow so fast we would like you to plant one for us that will reach up to the sky and into the new world. We have been here many days trying to find out how we can get up there."

"Yes," said the chipmunk, "I do know how to plant trees, but I cannot be very sure and promise you that I could make it grow up to reach the sky, but for your sake I will try, so let us pray to our gods who really have power."

They filled up their pipes and smoked again, to carry their earnest prayers to the gods. After this was done, the little chipmunk reached into his bag for his tree seeds. "This," he said, "is a spruce. We will try it first." He put it in his mouth and sang four of his magic songs. Then he took it out and set it in the ground in front of him, watching it very closely. Again he reached into his little bag and drew out his little rattle of sea shells with which he sang over his planted seed. Soon the tree began to grow out of the ground, and when it was about three inches high, he spit all over it and around the roots. With that it began to grow faster. Now, he kept this up as he was singing and his mouth began to get awfully dry so he asked for some water to increase the moisture in himself. Finally the tree was as high as a man stood and when it got this high he would run up on it and with his little paws would pull it upward at the very top. With songs and pulling it up, the tree was growing very fast indeed. The little creature kept this up till it had grown to its full height, but it did not reach the sky.

"I have done my best," said the chipmunk. "The tree will grow no more."

The high hopes of the chief sank again because the tree did not reach the opening up in the sky.

"Being called to help you," said the chipmunk, "I will try again, so keep your hopes and do not be discouraged. I think it has weakened this tree making it grow too fast, so this time it will be a little slower."

And he reached into his little bag for another seed which was a fir-pine. This he planted, with the same performance as the first time. Again, the little tree began to grow and the chipmunk repeated his same songs with new and strong hopes that he might make it reach the hole in the sky. Going up on this tree he would take his sacred meal and at the very top, with his prayer, he would throw this meal upward as high as he could, hoping that this would make it grow up through the opening.

While he was busy growing his tree every man was smoking his pipe and they were making their earnest prayers from their very hearts. Finally the chipmunk came back down to the ground again and said, "My tree has stopped growing again, although it has passed the first one by four men's height, but be not discouraged, I will try again. First, I must have prayer."

He reached into his bag and out he brought his little pipe and smoked. While he was smoking he kept a seed in his mouth which was a long-needle pine. When he had finished he set the seed in the ground again, and started his performance in the same manner with all the hopes of making it reach the sky, but this was also in vain, though it did pass the two first trees.

Now not only the chipmunk, but all the rest of the people were very much troubled and crying in their hearts to think that the trees had failed to reach the opening in the sky. The chipmunk, with a broken heart, filled up his little pipe and smoked, thinking very hard of what he could do next, because he thought himself powerless and knew that only his gods had unlimited power so with his smoking he prayed the gods for more wisdom. He could see that every heart was sad for the men were sitting around with their heads down upon their folded arms over their knees.

A thought came to him now, so he slowly raised his head and said, "We are all very sad but I will try again, so I wish to ask you from your very hearts if there is someone here who is not very willing to go and hates to leave behind the ones he loves or there may be some of you that still have evil thoughts in your hearts. All this work and many sleepless nights are getting heavy on our father, our chief. We must confess ourselves to him and to our gods that we will do right and will try to live the right kind of life in the upper world."

"We are all true," said they, "If we were not true we would not have stayed to this day with our chief."

The chipmunk left them and went to a place where the bamboo tree grows." Here he took a little shoot of a bamboo plant and with this he brought a tiny piñon shell full of water. These he set on a small basket tray and smoked his pipe over it, which was his earnest prayer. Others followed in the same manner. When this was done he put the piñon shell of water in the ground, at an arm length deep and on top of it he planted the bamboo shoot and he covered it up. He took his sacred corn meal in his right hand and stood over the plant and said his prayers in silence. Then he threw the meal high up toward the sky. Then the others followed one by one.

"Now," he said, "this being the last plant I know that will grow high we must give all our hearts to our gods that they may believe and answer our prayers and make this tree grow up through the opening in the sky."

When all their preparations were made and their sacred corn meal was thrown up toward the sky, the two birdmen started to sing their magic songs and the rest all joined with them because by that time, they knew the songs so that they could follow along with them. After the songs were ended, the little chipmunk ran up the tree and when he got to the top he pulled on it and he ran back four times up into that tree. Then he came down and filled up his pipe and started smoking.

He was always keeping time with the singing and he knew just when to run up the tree, and he just kept this performance up till the tree was high enough, and still they were singing and then, while they were singing, they asked the four other birds that had made their attempt to go up into the sky to find the opening, to fly up and see how high the tree had gone up, because by that time, the little chipmunk was tired, he couldn't run up the high tree again.

Now these birds, that is, the eagle and the hawk and the swallow bird and the shrike, made their trip up into the sky to the top of this tree four times and each time, when they came back they told the people that it was coming nearer to the opening. Toward the last, it was only the shrike that could go up and he made this trip up four times. But the last trip he made he stayed up on the top limb, and with him on the top limb the tree went through the opening. Of course, the old shrike felt very safe because he knew he could come back down, resting on the limbs of the tree.

When he came down he told the people that the tree had gone through the opening. Now the chipmunk was very glad that it had gone through, and of course you know that he was overjoyed. Then the chipmunk told them that it would be rather impossible to climb up on the tree. He told them that this tree was hollow inside and he started to gnawing on the bottom of the tree to cut an opening into it. While he was gnawing away all the men circled around the little fire and started their prayers again by smoking. After all this was done the chief said that as it was rather late in the day they would start their prayers and songs for the people at dawn. Now they were all very anxious to see the morning come and before it did come the chief had appointed two birds—the eagle and the swallow, to be on the look-out, so that no wicked people might pass.

Now on this day, before they started out, the chief said to the wise men that they must give an order for some kind of a guard that would hold back the bad people and the witches and wizards that would try to steal their way into the reed with the rest of the people. So the chief told the wise men to make their pahos for each four directions. These were to represent the closing of all the different trails from all directions. When these were made he sent out the One Horned Society or priests who were supposed to guard the North and West, and the Two Horned priests to guard the South and East. When they got to the four directions they made four lines out of sacred corn meal about six feet long and on both ends of the lines they set a paho falling backward—not toward the bamboo. Whoever steals their way into the bamboo and crosses this line will perish, which means that they will drop dead. Of course, many people tried to cross from different directions and were found dead.

This is how two of the societies or religions were started; *Kwakant* (One Horned Society) and *A-alt* (Two Horned Society), which are still in existence today. Whoever came to the bamboo by the set path came safely to the chief, to join in going to the Upper World.

The time came for them to sing their calling songs and before they started to sing they renewed their altar on which they had laid their prayer offerings. They made four of these prayer offerings and set them up on four sides of the tree to hold it up. These prayer offerings were about the span of a man's hand. When they started to sing they had to sing around the altar and the two birds were watching the opening at the bottom of the tree so in case the wicked people should start to come through they could drive them away. The two birds were appointed because they had sharp claws. When they started to sing their calling song, being a magic song, it took effect and they found the names of men who were in this ceremony following one another because the calling song as it began, named all the wise men who were serving in the ceremony. Before long the people were coming up one after another—that is, one family after another family.

When the people were gathered there, the chief had his prayer offering ready and at the foot of the tree he set this little prayer offering down in front of it. Then with his sacred corn meal he made a line pointing into it and then he walked in and his family followed and the rest of the royal families came after him, like the family of the village crier and the families of the others who had a high position, such as the high priest.

As they were going up through the tree the shrike started outside, because he was rather light and he could rest on the limbs. They didn't know how far they were going up. It took them quite a long while and the chief was rather anxious to get up to the top and after a long time they finally came up to the opening. When the chief got up there the shrike was waiting for him and when he crawled out of the tree the rest followed and as some of these people came out they started to sing the same songs that they were singing down at the bottom. These songs were limited and they were only to be sung four times, because they were awfully long songs. In a ceremony like this everybody was so anxious to get to the top it didn't seem so long and before all the people were through, the songs were ended and there were still some more people gathered around the tree. Then everywhere there was trouble down below, for those who hadn't been able to get up while the songs were being sung had to stay at the bottom, because the ceremony couldn't be sung any more.

Then the One Horned Priests who remained below had to cut the tree down for fear that someone might steal their way up, so they cut down the tree and this tree still had some people in it, so that is why the bamboo is jointed—because the people in there stuck in the tree and the tree kind of shrunk in between them.

CHAPTER II
MASAUWU

Now the chief was pleased to be on top, but of course, he was rather kind of suspicious for fear that some witches or wizards might have come through. They found that there was sunshine and birds and rather a prosperous looking world—sun, grass, flowers, trees and everything else up above.

When they had been up a few days, the chief asked his people if any of them had brought up anything with them to eat, or seeds of any kind. They searched one another and they found some corn and of course it was rather late in the season to plant anything now, so they didn't plant, they lived on game and wild fruit and seeds of the different kinds of plants.

Before very long there was a little girl who took sick and died suddenly. When this little girl died the chief held a council to find out if they had brought up any witches with them. Finally one of the girls had to admit that she was one of them. Of course they were very much troubled over her and got ahold of her and tied her up and were ready to throw her back into the underworld. The girl didn't want to be thrown back into the underworld so she told them not to be troubled because after death you went back into that underworld and were safe, that you returned to your own people down there again.

They asked her to prove it. "Well," she said, "I can easily prove it if you come to the kiva (opening). We can look down and see the little dead girl playing around down there just as happy as she can be."

And so they went to the kiva hole and looked down and saw this little girl playing around with the rest of the children below. When the witch girl had proved this to the people the chief had to permit her to stay.

On the fourth night after they came up to the world on top, they saw a fire a little distance away and they wondered who it could be, so the next morning the chief sent his braves to see where the fire had been. No sign of fire was to be found, only huge footprints of a big man or a giant, for these footprints were larger than any living man's. The braves came back to the chief and told of what big footprints they had seen, and they were all very much frightened. The chief thought the only thing to do was to have a ceremony of prayer offerings or paho making and offer these to their neighbor, the giant, for fear that he might be a man of some power, who might do them harm someday.

The village crier was called to announce the day for this ceremony. When the people came to the chief they found him to be sad of heart and they all knew why he was so sad. The chief told his fellow men what he thought it was best they should do, that they might make these prayer offerings to the fire or whoever it was that had the fire. As usual they all smoked their pipes before they set to work to make their pahos. When all was done they put these offerings together on one plaque, which received their earnest prayers as they smoked their pipes, and all this was done before it was taken to their strange neighbors.

Before it was taken over, the chief called for volunteers, to see who would step forward to take these prayer offerings to the being at the fire. They were to be taken at night and someone would have to carry it who was very brave. Four young men offered themselves and said they would take the offering over to the fire for among the Hopi four was the limit, and they were permitted to go.

Going over with the tray of prayer offerings they saw at first in the distance only a faint light and they were very much afraid. Coming closer, they could see someone sitting by the fire and facing away from them and they could only see the back of his head. This head was of rather a great size, like the biggest squash, and there was no hair on it. As they came closer they were more and more frightened, but at last they got to him. He would not turn his face toward the fire, so they called to him and asked him who he was, but he would not answer. They called to him a second time and he refused again to answer them. They called to him a third time, and again they received no answer. They called again, a fourth time, and asked him if he had some other language and did not understand them. Then he answered and said he was surprised to see that they had come to his fire because no one had ever gotten so near to him before.

When he said this he turned around toward the light and his face was all bloody and he had a mask on; his head was big and his mask was terrible looking. These four men were very much frightened and all felt something creeping back of their heads. Finally they got over their spell and told him what they had brought him, which the chief had sent over with his wishes that he would be their good friend and neighbor and not try to make them any trouble. They handed him the tray of pahos which he gladly received and was very much pleased with them, and he said that he prized them very highly.

Then he told these young men who he was. He was their god—the god of the Upper World, and it all belonged to him. Although being the god of the Upper World, he could not walk about in the day time, but only at night by the light of the fire. So he told these young men to tell their chief who he was—that he was now his god, who walked in the dark and is called the Masauwu. He was the god of death and life. He told the young men to tell the chief not to be afraid, that he being the god of death, whoever died would go to him first and he would show him back to the underworld by way of the kiva, through which they had come out.

When the young men went back to the chief, they told him the man at the fire received his offering and prized it very highly as it had been a long time since he had received any offering of pahos like that. This was the first time they had ever seen this man who said he was their god and ever since he has been worshipped by the Hopi. Since he told the people he was the god of death, they always go to him when they go on the warpath and ask him to paralyze their enemies with fear so that they may be victorious.

CHAPTER III
HOW THE MOCKING BIRD GAVE THE PEOPLE MANY LANGUAGES

AFTER awhile the chief said that they must move away from the kiva for fear that some of his people might become discouraged in some way, or lose courage and want to go back. They might die or want to die, so he didn't like to be near the kiva for fear the people might be going back and looking down toward their old home.

Even though the Chief had decided to move the people away from the kiva he was very much troubled and wondered how the kiva should be regarded by them, whether it should be thought of with apprehension and fear. So the chief called his wise men together to consult them on his ideas regarding this matter, but none of these men could give him any help or find him an answer. They could only ask him what he had in mind, saying that whatever the chief wished, their gods may consent to fulfill. "Very well," said their chief, "let us make some pahos and with these offerings we will ask the big waters to come and cover up the kiva and that will make it impossible for anyone to go back there."

When all these were made the young men were asked to take them to the southwest, toward *Patuwakachi* (the ocean) and at a good distance away from the kiva these pahos were set with the wishes and prayers of the chief that the waters may only come as far as the spot where the offerings were placed. Now every day, for four days the young men were sent back to this place where they had put these pahos to see if there were any signs of moisture or the coming of *Paso* (the roaring waters). Now every day the water was seen to be creeping up on these pahos and at the end of the fourth day the people began to feel the damp air. Then the big wind came and it kept up for many days and at last *Paso* had come and it had covered up all the land around the kiva so that no one could reach it. This was, of course, a very fearful thing to all the people.

Of course, no one knows how long they lived around that place, but after a great many years they increased and they started to have more trouble among themselves. The chief was afraid that something might happen again so he had a council with his men once more, and he asked them what should be done. One of the men said that the only thing that he thought of was, if they only could speak different languages and learn to eat different kinds of food from one another, they might start away or become parted in many divisions.

"Why," said the chief, "how could we do this?"

Someone said, "Well, don't we have the mocking bird who knows many songs and why shouldn't he give us many different languages?"

"Well," said the chief, "I think that is a very good idea."

Then he asked the men to come the next day so that they could make their prayer offerings for the mocking bird. So the next day the men came over with their trays and some materials with which to make their prayer offerings. They started work that morning and kept on until late in the afternoon. When all their prayer offerings were finished, the crier called out for the men to bring him their presents of food for them all to eat. After they finished their meal they started singing the calling songs for the mocking bird, and at the end of four songs the mocking bird came.

When he came he asked them why he was being so anxiously called. The chief answered him and said, "It is because we are in trouble and we wish to have some changes made, if it would be possible." Then the mocking bird asked what kind of changes.

"Well," said the chief, "would it be possible that we, living here as one people, could be given different languages?"

The mocking bird said, "It can be done."

The chief asked, "How soon can you do it?"

The mocking bird said that it would take overnight to give them different languages. The mocking bird asked the chief if he would like to speak some other different language, but the chief said he would rather keep his own language.

Well, that night it was only the chief and the mocking bird who stayed up to see how this thing would work out. During the night the mocking bird went from camp to camp and at each camp he would take something out of the fireplace and then turn right around and bury something in the fireplace again. He had a sort of buckskin pouch and whatever he took out of the fireplace he put into this pouch and he was holding on tight to this pouch for fear that something would escape out of there. Just about dawn the mocking bird finished his job. He took his buckskin pouch to the chief and told the chief to dig a hole in the ground. The chief did this and the mocking bird told him to put the pouch in the hole and bury it there and build a fire over it. Now when the morning came, the people woke up with different languages and they couldn't understand one another.

They were very much troubled because they couldn't understand one another and they came up to the chief and the chief couldn't make them understand. The mocking bird was the only one that could understand, so he was the interpreter.

"Well," said the chief, "you are a pretty wise bird. Now you and I will travel the same direction toward the rising sun and the sun may be our god, great and wise. With its light we can see and walk. Wherever this place is where the sun rises, I would like to see who will get there first for there we may learn who is our true god. If not, the sun itself is our god for there must be some spirit, somewhere, that really does look after us. If either you or I should get to the sun first, the great star will appear and many other stars will fall from the heavens, by which those who are still on the journey will know that one of us has reached the journey's end. Then the one who has arrived with his people must settle down and look forward to meeting his brother when he comes with wisdom and truth that he may teach the true religion of god."

CHAPTER IV
THE HOPI DECIDE TO SEEK A NEW HOME. HOW CERTAIN CLANS RECEIVED THEIR NAMES

ALL THIS time while the people were together, they learned to eat some of the wild seeds besides corn and different kinds of fruit and wheat. The mocking bird asked the chief to get all the different kinds of foodstuffs together and call the people to come and gather there, and decide and choose their food, or the chief food, that they wished to live on as they traveled along. Of course in those days the chief had charge of all the foodstuffs.

So he asked the people to gather all this food together and when they had gotten all they could collect he sent word out for no more people to come. When everything was gathered in, the chief sent word for the people to come together. Of course, all this time the mocking bird was still with them, because they could not go without him.

When the people came the chief asked them to look this foodstuff over and choose what they would like to take along in case they wanted to separate and travel along in different directions. Now that the mocking bird had given the people different languages and they couldn't understand each other they thought it would be best to separate.

After he had said all this the men shook hands to show that they were brothers and they started out on the race for the same point, as they were both anxious to learn and to find out who is the true God. Before they parted they said they would start out on their journey on the fourth day from that time, but during these three days the people of these two men and the women folk were getting ready the foodstuff for them to take along. Of course each of them had quite a number of people besides just their families.

On the fourth day all the tribes came together—Navajo, Supai, Paiute, Apache, Zuni, Utes and the Bahana. When they came up, the chief had all the different kinds of seeds of corn and grain, of melon and fruit, laid out for them to choose. Then he asked the different tribes to step forward and take their choice.

The Navajo slipped forward hurriedly and picked out the largest ear of corn, which he thought was the wise thing to do. But the chief and the others knew that the long ear of corn could not last long and was not easily raised. Afterward the rest of the tribes took their choice in turn.

The Hopi took the shortest ear of corn and also squash and beans. The Apache didn't take any, for they said they would rather live on game. Supai took some peaches—he preferred the fruit most. The Zuni took corn and wheat. Paiute didn't take any, he too said he would rather live on wild game and fruit. Utes didn't take any either. The Bahana (White man) took his choice last and was rather slow and considered well and finally he took some wheat which was not so heavy and he could carry more of it than the corn.

When they started out, for a few days they were kind of looking out for one another and keeping track of the time. They travelled on for many days and it got so that it was rather discouraging for they never had thought that the sun rose so far away; they thought that the sun rose only a short distance off. Finally they got so they didn't count the days any more.

As they traveled along, the first party came on a dead bear. They thought that they would name themselves the "Bear Clan" (*Hona-wunga*) and by this they could be recognized. They took the paws off the bear and took the flesh and bones out of them and stuffed them up with grass.

The second band came along and they too, found the dead bear. They had so many things to carry that they thought they needed some straps, so they took the hide off the bear and made straps of it. Then they thought they would take the name of "Strap Clan" (*Biaquoiswungwa*) by which they would be known.

Then it was many days before the third band came along. When they came to the dead bear it was all bones and the ribs were sticking up in the air and the bluebirds were sitting on them. Well, seeing the bluebirds there they thought they would call themselves the "Bluebird Clan", *Chosh-wunga*, by which name they would recognize each other. Then they went on, following the rest who were ahead of them. They must have known in some way that the two other clans were ahead of them.

Not very long after the "Bluebird Clan" had left this place, another band came along and they too found the dead bear. Inside of the skeleton of the bear was a spider web. Seeing the spider, they thought they would call themselves the "Spider Clan", *Koking-wungwa*.

Then the next band came along not very far behind them, and they too came to the same spot. They found gopher mounds around the skeleton of the bear so they thought they would call themselves the "Gopher Clan", *Mui-wunga*.

Maybe a few years later, another band came up and they too came to the same place and found that the skeleton of the bear was all in pieces. They found the skull with the greasy eye cavities, and they thought they would call themselves the *Wikurswungwa* Clan, "The greasy eye cavities of the skull." (Clan now extinct.)

These groups were all going eastward, toward the rising sun and of course, the man who was to be the Bahana, went on and got ahead.

As they were following one another, of course they all had it in mind to see the Eastern Star. Their brother, Bahana, had gone on and they thought he might be held up somewhere and they hoped to get ahead of him for they all hoped they would reach the rising sun first. Of course, out of all these clans the Bear Clan was ahead. Each clan wished to get ahead. One day the Spider Clan came upon a spider lying outside of its hole, and of course the leaders stopped and wondered if this spider could speak to them. So the chief called his people and they all gathered around the spider, wondering at it. Finally the Spider Woman spoke to them.

She called them her children and grandchildren. Then she said that if they needed to be helped she could help them. They said they would like to be helped, because they rather thought they were getting away behind the rest of the people. So the Spider Woman said that they would have to stay with her a few days and that she would get them something to travel with so they could go on faster. They said they would like to travel faster because on account of the children they were getting behind. So the Spider Woman asked them if they would like something to ride on so they wouldn't have to travel on foot, and they said they would.

"Well," she said, "I can make you a tame animal" that would carry your stuff and probably you can have him pack your things and you can walk behind him. If you don't carry any thing on your back you might travel faster."

"Well," the man said, "what could you make it of?"

The Spider Woman said "It has to be a part of you, so you go to that little room with the jar of water and take a bath and whatever rolls off your body—all that dirt—you gather it up and bring it to me."

So this man took a jar of water and went into a little room and started to take a bath. Of course, you know, having travelled many days thinking that he would get to the rising sun, why he never did stop to think about taking a bath and he was awful dirty. All afternoon he spent rubbing himself and all that dirt began to roll off of him. When he got through and gathered it up he almost had a handful. He came out and handed this to the Spider Woman and wondered what sort of an animal it would make and how big it would be, because he thought the dirt that rolled off himself wasn't big enough to make an animal of any kind.

Then the Spider Woman went to work and she brought out a little white robe. She laid this down and put the lump of dirt on it and covered it up with the robe and folded it over. Then she sang the magic songs. Every once in a while she would peek in under this cover and see if it was coming to life, and finally the thing started to move. The Spider Woman finished her songs. She took the little cover off and there was a little gray burro. Well, the Spider Woman told these people that they would have to stay there four days because in four days this little animal would then be strong enough to travel.

Every day the Spider Woman would feed this little animal something and wrap him up. Being a wise old woman, she would feed it some of her medicine—magic stuff—rubbing its legs to give it strength. Finally, in four days, the animal was ready to travel. The people packed up the burro with their stuff and they went on. Well, they found it was much easier to have something packing their stuff than to be packed up themselves.

Having made a burro for these people, this same Spider Woman made a man with knowledge and instructed him to go after these people and help them along, to train animals for them that they might catch up with brother Bahana. But not following the Spider Woman's instructions, this man stole the little burro and went on himself, thinking that he would get ahead of the Bahana and reach the point of the rising sun first. So one day these poor Hopis could not find their animal and they looked for many days. Finally, they found somebody's tracks driving the burro. He had funny shoes and whoever he was, he had slipped up on them and stolen their animal. Now they were made sad because they had to pack their own stuff again. Later, they came upon another Spider Woman who told them that this man was a Castilian who had stolen their burro.

By this time these people had almost forgotten about the rest of the Hopi and they hadn't heard of where they were all this time. They were traveling away behind and they were rather slow because they would stop to cultivate the land and raise corn to supply them for a few years. They thought that they would build houses and make pottery by which they would mark this land as they went along, because they believed the day would come when their brother would find the rising sun and that they would all come back this way with more power and more knowledge. Of course, they would be true to their brother, but there may be others who would come back with him and they would be the ones who would try to cheat him out of the land, so in order to have some kind of mark in this country they built homes and made pottery.

CHAPTER V
HOW THE HOPI SELECTED SHUNG-OPOVI FOR THEIR HOME

THE Hopis had forgotten about the other tribes by this time and did not know where they were. They were hoping to see the Eastern Star so that they could settle down and not travel any more. Well, finally the Bear Clan did see the Eastern Star and they were ready to settle down, but they didn't know just where would be a good place for them. They thought that they would do better cultivating by depending on rain, so they went out onto the Painted Desert to Shung-opovi (the place by the spring where the tall weeds grow). Being out here in such a desolate place they thought that they would be safe from other people, who would not think that they had anything worth taking.

By that time the other Hopis were down around the vicinity of Sunset Crater, Canyon Diablo and the Little Colorado River.

After a good many years these other Hopis heard of the Bear Clan being out at Shung-opovi, so the Strap Clan who were settled along Canyon Diablo, thought they would go out and join the Bear Clan. So they started out. When they did start out they stopped along the ridge below Ma-teuvi, which is now called Big Burro Spring. From there they sent off a messenger to Shung-opovi to tell the Chief that his brothers, the Strap Clan, would like to join him.

When the messenger came to the Chief of Shung-opovi and told him what the Strap Clan leader wished to do, he could not very well answer his message just then. So he sent word back that he would like to have the Strap Clan chief come himself. When the Strap Clan leader heard this word he went up to Shung-opovi with his bag of tobacco and his pipe.

Of course, in those days, they had guards that were always on the lookout for someone coming, for fear it might. be an enemy. Well, this man was seen coming and the Chief was notified. He knew who it was, the man being alone, so he went out to meet him and he met him at the place called Teuviovi (point that runs out south of Shung-opovi Day School). When they met there, they greeted one another by smoking their pipes. After they had smoked their pipes, the Strap Clan leader told the chief of the Bear Clan how he had followed his trail and that he had taken his clan name from the same dead bear that he had. So for that reason, he considered himself as his brother and he would like to join his establishment, because he thought being of the same clanship the Bear Clan was not any greater than the Strap Clan was. So the Bear Clan told him he could go back and bring his people.

Well, the Strap Clan leader went back and told his people this good news and asked the people to get ready, as they would start for Shung-opovi in four days. On the fourth day they started out and when they got to Shung-opovi they were very well received.

When the Strap Clan entered the village they thought they would have the same rights as the Bear Clan but the Bear Clan did not like the way the Strap Clan felt about their rights and the way they were acting, so finally they had to have a council and talk this over. They decided the Bear Clan would give the Strap Clan a chance to become a royal clan and to rule the village. Of course, after this the Strap Clan was always looking forward to this agreement. Now later, the other clans began to drift in. When they came up to the town they would send word up to the chief and the chief would usually send for the leader to come to see him, because it was not his business to go down and meet the people. They had to come up before the chief. He would always ask the leader about his religious rites or ceremonies—of how he had been serving his people in the way of prosperity, if his ceremonies have any effect on the gods and if his ceremonies would bring rain. And of course this chief would have to tell what he did to bring rain or how he did it. Then, if the chief thought he was rather bragging about himself, or exaggerating his ceremonies, he would tell him to stay away, because if he could take care of his people that way, he could get along all right by himself. The chief knew that no human would have such power and that he had to ask the gods or make prayers for rain to make his crops grow.

Many a time some clan leader had to go up to the chief four times before he was permitted to enter with his people. Every time when a band or clan was received, the chief would allot them so much land. The last few clans to arrive were just the common class of people. They didn't have a high priest, or ceremonies of any kind, and they were the ones that had a hard time getting into the village. They were not alloted any land. They wished to have land also, so they asked the chief. The chief asked them what they could do—or what right they had to be given that land. They said that they were willing to have the land on the edges and they would guard his people and keep away the enemies, so since they told him all this, they were given all the outside land which was not allotted to any other clan.

After this was all settled, another clan came along and they were also a common class, and the chief asked them if they had any ceremonies of any kind by which they lived, or by which they prayed to the gods to bring them rain. They said no, they didn't have any and they told him they didn't have any time for ceremonies, they were nothing but warriors and had to fight their way up there, for the country was full of other tribes that were enemies of these people. So the chief said that if they were warriors and had to fight their way up there, they would be his braves. This was the Sun Forehead Clan. Then the chief went to the Parrot Clan (*Gash-wunga*) and asked them if they would give up some of their land to the Sun Forehead Clan, that they too might take their place in guarding the chief's rights and those of his people. The Parrot Clan was very glad to do this, so from then on the Sun Forehead Clan had to be out first if enemies made an attack.

Then, later on, another clan came along, the Sun Clan. They too were without a religion and ceremonies. This Sun Clan was given the same treatment as the clan before them and the Sun Forehead Clan gave up part of their land that the Sun Clan might guard the rights of the people, so to this day, their lands are still on the edge of the Hopi lands.

CHAPTER VI
HOW THE CROW CLAN ARRIVED AND SETTLED AT MISHONGNOVI

LONG before this time the Crow Clan had made a little settlement at what is called the first Mishongnovi, on the west side of Quang-oufovi Mesa, or Bald Mesa. The leader of this clan was called Mishong, or Black Man, on account of his dark color. They lived there for awhile, but they were much troubled, for there was some sort of a great reptile that lived there, which seemed as if it had no end to it, and sometimes in the morning he would be all over the place, the great coils of him going round and round the little houses on the steep terraced mesa. He had one little pair of wings and Tok-chi-i, he was called. On account of that snake they were having great trouble. It was rather harmless, but they were afraid of it. When this great snake gathered himself together he formed a shape like a plaque and then he would take off into the air and was gone for a long time, and it might be months before he returned again, but when he did return he piled himself up on that little village again. On account of him the people left the place and went to Shung-opovi and settled down about three-fourths of the way to the top of the Mesa. When the Shung-opovi people found out that there were only seven families of them there they called their place the Seventh Point—Chung-ait-tuika.

While living at this place they were constantly asking the Shung-opovi chief if they could join with his people, but he refused them every time, because they were a dark colored people. Of course, they didn't have any land to farm and what little gardening they did was on the bench where there was only a few inches of dirt on top of the rocks. Finally the Mishongnovi leader went to the Shung-opovi chief again.

Now about this time Walpi was established, and when the Shung-opovi people heard about it they decided they would let the Mishongnovi people go to guard the Corn Rock which was a very important shrine.

So the chief of Shung-opovi said, "If you want to become a part of my people, I have a shrine by the Corn Rock and I need someone to take care of it. If you wish to be a part of my people you must settle there."

The chief of Shung-opovi continued, "The eastern star has come up so that we are expecting the Bahana, our savior, a white man. We want to know him when he comes, so I delegate the Crow Clan to look for the Bahana. The Bahana, our savior, will do away with all evil people. But if the Bahana is not the true Bahana it will be your duty to make away with him." So Mishong and his people settled by the Corn Rock, founding Mishongnovi, and the Crow Clan has handed down the idea that they are the ones to look for the Bahana. Other clans joined this pueblo so the Crow Clan became the royal family of Mishongnovi. When Mishong's people were settled there they were given some land to the southeast.

Now the chief of Walpi thought they were taking some of his land, so the Chief of the Shung-opovi went to Walpi and told the Chief that he had the right to give the people that much land as he was the first one to serve them. So then they made a boundary line from one of the points on the North Mesa to the South Mesa. The North Mesa is called Po-noteu-we (shrine that looks like a fat person). The South Mesa is called Aku-haivi (meaning "a little pool or deep rock tank" and here they could easily dip water with a ladle (*aku*) which always hung there.) This seemed to be satisfactory to both sides, so they settled on that question of the boundary line.

About this time all the other villages were just beginning to be established, like Awatovi, and the others on the Jeddito, and it was found that the Awatovi people were speaking the same dialect as the Mishongnovi people. Of course at that time there was nobody at Shipaulovi.

CHAPTER VII
HOW A FAMILY QUARREL LED TO THE FOUNDING OF ORAIBI

LIKE all the other people, the Shung-opovi chief and his brothers were usually having some kind of trouble or argument over something, and about this time he found out that his younger brother was too bold. He was rather taking too much authority upon himself and didn't have much respect for the other people. He never would do much of anything in the way of work, but he would always be down in the fields when the crops were ripe and he helped himself to the things the other people had grown. Since he was one of the royal family no one had a right to say anything to him, and he was always grabbing corn from other people's fields at the time of the harvest and that was where he got his provisions, for he didn't grow anything himself.

Now the people were rather tired of this and they were all turning against him, but no one dared say anything. One day they had baked sweet corn and the men were there husking it, and this man came down and picked out as much as he could carry of the best corn the men had. It happened that his brother, the Chief, was there at the time and his brother, having the same right or being a little above him, called him down. Then all the other men thought that was their chance to say something to him and they all called him down. That hurt him more than anything else and he left all the corn right there and went home.

When night came on he left Shung-opovi. The next morning he was missing and no one knew where he had gone and from then on, they were always looking for him and would send out searching parties but they never could find him. Nobody ever heard anything about him. All the other villages were asked if he had gone to one of them, but he was not in any of them.

One day they went out hunting and at that time Third Mesa was a hunting place where they hunted cottontails among the rock. Now while they were there hunting, they found this man. He was living in one of the little caves. His name was Ma-chito. When they found him they tried to get him to talk but he wouldn't speak to them, so they tried to bring him back home but he would not go with them.

When they got home they told his wife that her husband was over on the mesa and asked her to go and see if she could get him to come home. The next day she went but he told her he would never return to Shung-opovi—that he had left his people for good. He wanted to see how his brother would get along without him, because he considered that he himself had witchcraft power and that it was he that knew all the different songs and all the ceremonies that were being carried on at that time. His wife made four trips over there but she could not get him to come home, so she decided to go over and join him.

So when she got there, they went up on top of the mesa and built up there. From then on, in the other villages, whoever was mistreated or got mad at something went over there to live. When other clans drifted in, Ma-chito didn't have many questions to ask of them, but just brought them in, for he wanted to get ahead of his brother and have more people in a short time.

CHAPTER VIII

HOW THE SPANIARDS CAME TO SHUNG-OPOVI, HOW THEY BUILT A MISSION, AND HOW THE HOPI DESTROYED THE MISSION

IT MAY have taken quite a long time for these villages to be established. Anyway, every place was pretty well settled down when the Spanish came. The Spanish were first heard of at Zuni and then at Awatovi. They came on to Shung-opovi, passing Walpi. At First Mesa, Si-kyatki was the largest village then, and they were called Si-kyatki, not Walpi. The Walpi people were living below the present village on the west side. When the Spaniards came, the Hopi thought that they were the ones they were looking for—their white brother, the Bahana, their savior.

The Spaniards visited Shung-opovi several times before the missions were established. The people of Mishongovi welcomed them so the priest who was with the white men built the first Hopi mission at Mishongovi. The people of Shung-opovi were at first afraid of the priests but later they decided he was really the Bahana, the savior, and let him build a mission at Shung-opovi.

Well, about this time the Strap Clan were ruling at Shung-opovi and they were the ones that gave permission to establish the mission. The Spaniards, whom they called Castilla, told the people that they had much more power than all their chiefs and a whole lot more power than the witches. The people were very much afraid of them, particularly if they had much more power than the witches. They were so scared that they could do nothing but allow themselves to be made slaves. Whatever they wanted done must be done. Any man in power that was in this position the Hopi called *Tota-achi*, which means a grouchy person that will not do anything himself, like a child. They couldn't refuse, or they would be slashed to death or punished in some way. There were two *Tota-achi*.

The missionary did not like the ceremonies. He did not like the Kachinas and he destroyed the altars and the customs. He called it idol worship and burned up all the ceremonial things in the plaza.

When the Priests started to build the mission, the men were sent away over near the San Francisco peaks to get the pine or spruce beams. These beams were cut and put into shape roughly and were then left till the next year when they had dried out. Beams of that size were hard to carry and the first few times they tried to carry these beams on their backs, twenty to thirty men walking side by side under the beam. But this was rather hard in rough places and one end had to swing around. So finally they figured out a way of carrying the beam in between them. They lined up two by two with the beam between the lines. In doing this, some of the Hopis were given authority by the missionary to look after these men and to see if they all did their duty. If any man gave out on the way he was simply left to die. There was great suffering. Some died for lack of food and water, while others developed scabs and sores on their bodies.

It took a good many years for them to get enough beams to Shung-opovi to build the mission. When this mission was finally built, all the people in the village had to come there to worship, and those that did not come were punished severely. In that way their own religion was altogether wiped out, because they were not allowed to worship in their own way. All this trouble was a heavy burden on them and they thought it was on account of this that they were having a heavy drought at this time. They thought their gods had given them up because they weren't worshiping the way they should.

Now during this time the men would go out pretending they were going on a hunting trip and they would go to some hiding place, to make their prayer offerings. So today, a good many of these places are still to be found where they left their little stone bowls in which they ground their copper ore to paint the prayer sticks. These places are called *Puwa-kiki*, cave places. If these men were caught they were severely punished.

Now this man, Tota-achi (the Priest) was going from bad to worse. He was not doing the people any good and he was always figuring what he could do to harm them. So he thought out how the water from different springs or rivers would taste and he was always sending some man to these springs to get water for him to drink, but it was noticed that he always chose the men who had pretty wives. He tried to send them far away so that they would be gone two or three days, so it was not very long until they began to see what he was doing. The men were even sent to the Little Colorado River to get water for him, or to Moencopi. Finally, when a man was sent out he'd go out into the rocks and hide, and when the night came he would come home. Then, the priest, thinking the man was away, would come to visit his wife, but instead the man would be there when he came. Many men were punished for this.

All this time the priest, who had great power, wanted all the young girls to be brought to him when they were about thirteen or fourteen years old. They had to live with the priest. He told the people they would become better women if they lived with him for about three years. Now one of these girls told what the Tota-achi were doing and a brother of the girl heard of this and he asked his sister about it, and he was very angry. This brother went to the mission and wanted to kill the priest that very day, but the priest scared him and he did nothing. So the Shung-opovi people sent this boy, who was a good runner, to Awatovi to see if they were doing the same thing over there, which they were. So that was how they got all the evidence against the priest.

Then the chief at Awatovi sent word by this boy that all the priests would be killed on the fourth day after the full moon. They had no calendar and that was the best way they had of setting the date. In order to make sure that everyone would rise up and do this thing on the fourth day the boy was given a cotton string with knots in it and each day he was to untie one of these knots until they were all out and that would be the day for the attack.

Things were getting worse and worse so the chief of Shung-opovi went over to Mishongnovi and the two chiefs discussed their troubles. "He is not the savior and it is your duty to kill him," said the chief of Shung-opovi. The chief of Mishongnovi replied, "If I end his life, my own life is ended."

Now the priest would not let the people manufacture prayer offerings, so they had to make them among the rocks in the cliffs out of sight, so again one day the chief of Shung-opovi went to Mishongnovi with tobacco and materials to make prayer offerings. He was joined by the chief of Mishongnovi and the two went a mile north to a cave. For four days they lived there heartbroken in the cave, making pahos. Then the chief of Mishongnovi took the prayer offerings and climbed to the top of the Corn Rock and deposited them in the shrine, for according to the ancient agreement with the Mishongnovi people it was their duty to do away with the enemy.

He then, with some of his best men, went to Shung-opovi, but he carried no weapons. He placed his men at every door of the priest's house. Then he knocked on the door and walked in. He asked the priest to come out but the priest was suspicious and would not come out. The chief asked the priest four times and each time the priest refused. Finally, the priest said, "I think you are up to something."

The chief said, "I have come to kill you." "You can't kill me," cried the priest, "you have no power to kill me. If you do, I will come to life and wipe out your whole tribe."

The chief returned, "If you have this power, then blow me out into the air; my gods have more power than you have. My gods have put a heart into me to enter your home. I have no weapons. You have your weapons handy, hanging on the wall. My gods have prevented you from getting your weapons."

The old priest made a rush and grabbed his sword from the wall. The chief of Mishongnovi yelled and the doors were broken open. The priest cut down the chief and fought right and left but was soon overpowered, and his sword taken from him.

They tied his hands behind his back. Out of the big beams outside they made a tripod. They hung him on the beams, kindled a fire and burned him.

CHAPTER IX
RETURN OF THE SPANIARDS TO HOPI COUNTRY. SHIPAULOVI FOUNDED AS A SANCTUARY

AFTER all this had happened the Hopi were sure that the Spaniards were going to come back and make an attack on them and they figured that they would be wiped out. The chief of Shung-opovi thought there should be someone saved who would keep a record of these happenings in the best way they could. Now just about that time the Sun Forehead Clan was admitted into the village. They came from Homolovi. The chief sent one of his relations of the Bear Clan and his family to Shipaulovi and with them he sent half of the Sun Forehead Clan. He told them that this Shipaulovi village would be recognized as an innocent town, and that whenever the Hopi were attacked by any of their enemies whoever wished to live, could go there.

After all this the chief just simply waited for the attack to come from the Spanish, for knowing that he was guilty, he would not hesitate to give himself up to the Spaniards.

He waited quite a long while about 20 years—but nobody knows just how long. Finally the Spanish came. When they did come, instead of going up to the village they camped about three-fourths of a mile below the old Shung-opovi town and the whole village was in terror. The chief went down to the camp to ask them if they had come then to be friends, or to destroy.

The captain of the army told him that they had only come for the guilty. Then the chief said that the whole village was guilty, because everybody that could had put a hand on the priest. Then the captain said that could not be, because there were a good many people in the village and he couldn't understand how everyone could have put a hand on the priest. Then the chief said, if he was guilty all the people were guilty for he was their chief and leader. The captain asked the chief to have all the men of the village descend down there, so the chief called his men to come. When all the men got there, the captain lined them up and then he asked the chief to pick out the men that were really guilty.

Before the chief said a word, the men declared they were all guilty; but the captain would not believe them. During all this excitement there was one Hopi had the heart to come out with the truth. He stepped out and said he didn't like to see all the men get killed, for some of them were too young. They might become good runners or warriors and have long lives to live.

This man turned around to the chief and accused him of simply sacrificing his men because he didn't want to be put to death alone. He said that if he saved some of these men or convinced the Spaniards that these men were not all guilty, he himself would be willing to take the place of the chief and be the leader of the people. He was a man of the Strap Clan, closely related to the Bear Clan to which the chief belonged. This man was angry to think that the chief would sacrifice his men for nothing.

Then after this man had said he would be the leader of the people, he asked the chief to step forward and be honest and point out the ones who were really guilty. But the chief still wasn't man enough to do it, and he was asked four times before he would pick out the guilty men. The men were those who held positions in different kinds of ceremonies. With the Hopi, things like the doing away with the priest are not discussed with the common people—only among the leaders.

When these men were picked out, their hands were tied behind them and they were taken prisoners with the chief. The man of the Strap Clan took his men back to the village and the people coming out to meet them and seeing these men, declared him the chief. The next morning the men that were taken prisoners were shot at sunrise. Then the captain sent word up to the village that if they wished to bury the dead they could come and do it, but the people would not go down for fear they might get killed, so they waited until the Spaniards went away.

The new chief took everything in his hands and went down with some of his men and buried the dead. Each man was buried with his possessions, turquoise and shell beads. In those days the father's relatives would give presents of pottery to be buried with the dead. So they were buried with all those things.

Now the people of Shung-opovi had lived in the same village until the Spanish came back. Then the Strap Clan leader led the people to the top of the mesa and founded the new Shung-opovi, for he was afraid if they stayed down below, there would be more Spanish attacks.

From then on the Strap Clan people were leaders in Shung-opovi. During the next few years things were very prosperous, but it happened that they failed again—another drought came. At this time the people held a council and made an agreement that every clan be given a chance to take their turn at leadership. So from then on, each clan took its turn and it finally came back to the Bear Clan (each clan held leadership for four years) and when their turn was up they refused to give it up for they claimed it was theirs originally. Since they refused to give up their leadership they have remained the royal family ever since.

About this time another company of Spanish soldiers came and old Mishongnovi was still inhabited at that time, for all the people had not yet moved up on top. They stopped on the other side of Mishongnovi and asked the chief if he would make an agreement to let them in. He refused them four times. Then the captain of the Spanish soldiers said he had to destroy their village. Of course the people were very much afraid then, for they had seen what had happened at Shung-opovi and how the Spanish had killed the leaders of the trouble over there. Shung-opovi was then partly in ruins for the people were carrying away the beams to build their new homes on top, but somehow the Spanish didn't make an attack that time but went away again."

After they had gone away the Mishongnovi people wanted to stop up their spring, called *Yo-niai-va* (Antelope Chipmunk), which was a good spring at that time. They closed it up and had a paho-making ceremony. After they made their prayer offerings every man spun some cotton and when this was done they selected four different kinds of pahos and then wrapped cotton yarn over them. It made a round roll, about 10 inches long and about eight inches in diameter. With this they blocked up the water hole. Then in front of it they put a plaque and sealed it up around the edges with sweet cornmeal mush. They did this so that if the Spanish ever came back they would find no water there. This spring was to be opened up when the good white man or his brother came back, but today nobody knows just where the spring really is.

When they had done this they started to move up on top of the mesa, but before they had all moved, the Spanish came back again. Finding no water where they had camped before, they went right into the village and destroyed it. No one was killed and the few people who were left escaped and moved up to the mesa top. Their, the Spanish tried to get to the new village on top, but there was no trail and the people had piled up stones which they rolled down on the Spanish so that they were unable to climb up.

Shipaulovi was pretty well established at this time, but was under a sub-chief of Shung-opovi, as Mishongnovi was too.

After all these happenings the chiefs of the three villages held a council and made an agreement that there should be a limited place where the next white man should stop. This place is where the Sunlight Mission now stands. It was put up to the Mishongnovi chief that it was to be his duty to look out for that. There was also another limited line—between Shipaulovi and Mishongnovi. If any attack should come from the outside on Mishongnovi, whoever wished to save his own life could go over to the Shipaulovi side, where they were not supposed to be touched. Shipaulovi was the place of safety and was not supposed to have any blood stain. No one there could fight and no one was supposed to fight them.

For a long time these two villages were under Shung-opovi, but finally it was too much for them to handle, on account of the great number of ceremonies they were supposed to have. Finally, Mishongnovi was given its freedom. Shipaulovi today is not altogether under Shung-opovi, but the people still go to Shung-opovi for their initiation ceremonies (*Wuwuchime*).

CHAPTER X
THE RETURN OF THE BAHANA, THE WHITE MAN

ALL THIS time the Hopi seemed to know that the real Bahana was coming, but they were warned to be careful and patient, for fear it might not be the true Bahana who would come after the Spaniard or Castilian. So if he ever did come they must be sure to ask him about his books, which they thought would contain his secrets, and it was said that the book of truth would not be on top, but at the very bottom, after all the other books. If he asked the Hopi for the privilege of teaching them his language and taught them how to write, they must be sure to ask that they would like to be taught in the book of truth, because if he was a true Bahana he would quickly consent to teach them of this book. For their belief is, that if he is not the one they are looking for he will refuse to teach them his religion. Now if they learned his religion they would compare it with their religion and ceremonies, and if these were alike they would know that the Bahana had been with them in the beginning.

Most everybody was anxious to see the Bahana come, for they were so afraid that he might not come during their lifetime and they would not be able to enjoy all the benefits that he was to bring back with him-for the Bahana was supposed to bring great knowledge with him. These people were telling their children that the Bahana was wise and with his inventions had reached the rising sun and was coming back to them again, for they had seen the big eastern star and that was a sign and they were waiting for him. Every grandfather and grandmother was telling their children that they were growing so old that they would not see the Bahana. They would tell their grandchildren to go out in the mornings before sunrise with sacred corn-meal to ask the sun to hurry the Bahana along so that he would come soon.

Well, I guess many years had passed, probably a century. You know, some were rather superstitious and they would say that when the Bahana came he would know who was practicing witchcraft and that he would know them by sight. They said that he was to come and make peace and do away with all evil so that there would be no more trouble. And so, for this reason, the people who had so much trouble were the most anxious to see him come.

Well, finally they heard that the Bahana was at Tsehotso (Navajo for Fort Defiance) which means "range of sharp-pointed rocks." He was calling for the Hopi chiefs to come to that place to meet him. Now at that time all the tribes were on hostile terms with one another and it was dangerous. The Hopi wanted to go and see what this Bahana looked like. The chiefs from all the villages went there and they told him if he was the true Bahana they would shake hands and lay down their weapons, for they had a "theory" that when the Bahana came there would be peace forever. Well, at this place they were given cloth of different kinds, flour and sugar and a few tools like axes and knives. That was the first time that they had ever tasted sugar. When they brought these things back home this caused much excitement in all the towns. Of course, they would have to go back and take more men with them but they were always afraid of attacks from the Navajos and the Paiutes. So the Hopis, knowing that the white man was at Fort Defiance and that he had promised to let his soldiers protect the friendly people, knew also that if they were attacked by the Navajos and fighting with them, the soldiers would come. So every time the Navajos made an attack the Hopis would have to fight and if they made a retreat they would follow them up. The Hopis got so that they were good fighters themselves. The Navajos were not much of fighters, for they made up war parties and went places looking for trouble. Well, when they were doing this they thought it was great fun. The Hopi said that if they sighted some hogans they would hide out in the day time and move up at night. These Hopis would have signals like the call of an owl (there are two different kinds of owls—hoot owl and small owl that makes a whistling noise) or a crow. During the night they would circle around the hogans and would signal back and forth imitating the owls or crows to see if the Navajos were all awake. They would surround the place and wait until sunrise before making an attack.

Some old men who used to tell about this said it was great fun and like chasing cottontails on a rocky hill. They (Navajos) would be so scared they couldn't run and all they had to do was to hit them on the head with a club. These old men said that when they had grown old, they knew what a great wrong they had done.

CHAPTER XI
HOW THE HOPI MARKED THE BOUNDARY LINE BETWEEN THEIR COUNTRY AND THAT OF THE NAVAJO

NOW with all this fighting and the Navajo coming in around them, the Hopi were always thinking of their boundary lines and of how they should be marked in some way. But how? What sort of a mark could they put that would be respected by other peoples? It must be something that both the Hopis and the Navajos would remember.

So just at this time there were two men at Walpi who were rivals over a woman named Wupo-wuti. Now both these men were looking for a chance to show this woman how brave and strong they were. Finally they thought of this boundary line and the "theory" of their people that it should be marked in such a way that everyone would always remember. So these two men thought that this was a chance for them to prove themselves and to really do something for their people at the same time. They thought they would plan a fight with the Navajos as near the boundary line as they could get and there they would sacrifice themselves and leave their skulls to mark the line. In this way they thought that they would prove that they were brave and good fighters and they would really be doing something for their people, and so it was agreed upon.

Then Masale (feathers crossed) said they would go to Fort Defiance. So they both made an agreement that they would go early in the fall. Tawupu (rabbit skin blanket) thought they were going alone, but later he found out that there was going to be a party going over. He thought they were sacrificing too many lives, but, of course, he had made the promise to this other man so that he could not tell on him or give him away at that time. The crier made an announcement that whoever wanted to go to Fort Defiance with this party was welcome, and that they must prepare themselves and be ready to go soon. Masale had a son named Hani and he loved him, so he thought that he would take him along. He figured that if he should be killed it might be best for the boy to die also. Of course, this being a time of war, everyone was asked to take his bows and arrows along. Masale asked his boy to come along and to be sure to make some new arrows. The boy, of course, being ignorant of his father's plans, was glad to go with them.

By this time the people had found out that the two rivals were going together to Fort Defiance, and they figured out that there was something going to happen—that they were going out to give themselves away, or sacrifice their lives.

The morning of the day they were starting out, one of the relatives of this boy, Hani, asked him if he was going along with his father and he said he was. This man said to the boy that it would be better for him not to go with them. But Hani said he was all ready and the man, being his father, he was going along with him.

"Well," this relative said, "if you are, I will warn you right now. Wherever you camp you want to be sure where you lay your weapons or your bows and arrows, for your life will be in danger." He told him never to lay his bow and arrows under his head, but that he must lay them at his feet. "Because," this man said, "if you are lying on your back with your bows and arrows at your feet and you are waked up suddenly you will jump up forward. Having your weapons there at your feet you will lay your hands on them every time." He also told him that he must try not to sleep too soundly; that he must remember he was in danger all the time.

Hani, after getting his warning, started out and was the last one to leave. At that time the trail was through Keams Canyon. When he was quite a ways through the canyon, an eagle flew over his head and it was flying low. He thought that if the eagle settled down somewhere on a rock he would kill it and take the feathers along in case he wanted to make some more arrows on the way, so he kind of hid himself in the brush. Finally the eagle landed on top of a rock and Hani crawled toward him and took a shot at him. He did get him and the bird fell from the rock. Hani ran over to the place and found that his eagle was a buzzard. This seemed kind of strange, for he really had seen an eagle. That made him sort of suspicious. He thought it might be a warning or witchcraft, but as he was on his way already, he couldn't very well turn back. Well, finally he came up with the party, in the late afternoon.

That night when they made their first camp he had the warnings in his mind and he couldn't sleep. Anyway, he must have fallen asleep for a while and when he opened his eyes he was wide awake. He heard two men talking but he didn't make any noise and pretended he was sound asleep. He recognized his father's voice and also the voice of the other man, Tawupu. He overheard Tawupu asking his father why he had brought his boy along and his father said he couldn't very well leave him behind because he loved him so dearly. He said that if his boy should refuse to come along with him he would back out too, and he said it would be better for both of them if they got killed. When the boy began to move the two men rushed back and crawled into their beds. Now, after Hani had overheard what the two men had said, he couldn't sleep.

From then on the boy was rather uneasy every night when they made camp. After they lay down to sleep he'd keep awake quite a while because he knew, then, what the two men were up to. All the rest of the party didn't seem to know anything about it. They were ignorant of the plans of the two men.

After several days on the road, they finally reached the place—Fort Defiance. There they were welcomed by the white man and were asked to stay several days with them. There were twelve or fifteen men in the party. Four being the sacred number of the Hopi, they decided to stay four days. On the fourth day, when they were getting ready to go back home, the Bahana gave them flour and sugar and coffee and different kinds of cloth, besides yarns.

So the next morning when they were ready to leave, every burro they had with them was pretty well packed. Before they left they were asked if they would like to have a guard to go along with them. In case they were in any danger, they would have someone to show that they were the friends of the white man and they were not to be harmed, but since they didn't see any signs of danger when they were coming over they refused to take a guard along. Having been granted all their wishes for things that they had wanted for so long, they were very happy when they left there.

They were two days on the road before they reached Ganado, and the night before they reached Ganado this boy, Hani, overheard the two men talking with some other man. This time there were three men sitting around the camp fire quietly smoking. The boy could not really understand just what they were saying because it was all in a whisper. Then , of course, he couldn't help but move and when he did, one man rushed off and the other two men went to bed. One man was an outsider, a Navajo. The next morning the boy was more suspicious than ever, but still he could not ask his father what this night meeting was about.

So that day they traveled all day (on the other side of Ganado). On this day camp was made rather early and they said they wanted to get settled before dark. So they got everything ready before the sun went down, which was northwest of Ganado in the red hills. They said that they would have a good supper that night, so they cooked a great deal of their food that they had gotten at Fort Defiance—with bacon and some beef that they had brought along. Having an early supper, they said they would go to bed soon and would get up early in the morning, for they figured on reaching home the next night.

This man, Masale, the boy's father, seemed very happy that night. Before going to bed they cut a lot of branches off the cedars and brush that was around and put them clear around the camp, as a windbreak, you might say. Against this they put their saddles and all the packs that they had. That night Hani kept awake quite a long time, but he could not stand it very long so he finally fell asleep.

During the night sometime, Hani thought that he was dreaming and that there was a heavy hail storm coming up for he thought that he heard the hail dropping. First he heard it dropping slowly and then faster. When he was wide awake he knew what was going on. They were being attacked and when he did come to, all the men were up. About this time his father spoke at the top of his voice in Apache, then in Navajo and then in Zuni. He was asking who it was that was attacking them. The boy did not forget where to have his bow and arrows every night, so when he did jump up he had his hands right on his bow. By this time arrows were coming from every direction. When Hani was well on his feet all the enemy rushed into the camp, and as this was during the night he did not know who was who. Anyway, he started on a run and they chased after him. It happened that some Navajo had a corn patch near there and in the corn patch he had some squash with very long vines. Hani thought the whole country was full of enemies, so he hid under the vines, breathless and excited. He heard his father make his last groan and he was very angry. Dead or alive, he decided to go back, but found himself with only a few arrows, two or three left. So he ran back to the camp and when he got there he found his father dead, with many arrows sticking in his body. His scalp was gone. He thought that before doing anything else he must find his arrows and he found them rolled up in his blanket. This little blanket was only half the size of a double saddle blanket. Now the enemy thought that he was one of their party so he was not shot at until he had shot at them. As the enemy followed him he ran backward, holding the little blanket in front of him to stop the arrows. The moon was just going down below the horizon and it was getting quite dark.

At first he did not realize that he had been shot, for being a good runner the enemy could not keep up with him, but when he got up to the hills they were rather too steep for him to climb, because he realized then that he was shot, one arrow in his stomach, one in his hip and one between his shoulders. He pulled out two, the one from his hip and the one from his stomach, but he couldn't reach the one in his back. Well, anyway, he thought himself dead when he started to crawl up the hill. When he was halfway up the hill he cried for his dear life and prayed to his gods that if he should die, some day his skull would be found there. He didn't know how many of the party were killed or saved; he didn't know whether they were all dead or not. When he said his prayers, he cried some more, but he couldn't cry very loud, for he'd rather die in peace than have the enemy find him and use a club on him.

As he was going up, it began to show that it was dawn. He could see the daylight over the horizon and he wished that he would not die. If the sun did come up in time, he believed that it would give him strength. Of course, he couldn't help from groaning as he crawled up, and then he heard someone speak to him from the top of the hill, which scared him nearly to death and he thought some enemy had headed him off, so he did not answer. The voice came again and it was in plain Hopi. It said, "Are you hurt badly?" And he said, "Yes." And then the other said, "Will you be able to make it up here?" But he said, "No." So this other man came down and helped him up. When they got up he recognized this man and it was a man by the name of Mai-yaro. Well, this man said to the wounded boy that they would try to travel on together, as he was not wounded. He had been in the party, but had got away safely.

Hani told him to go on and leave him alone for he was done for and was ready to die, but this other man refused to leave him. He said that if the enemy should head them off and follow them, he would be willing to die with him. So they went on walking slowly, and while they were going along, another man named Tochi (Moccasin) joined them. He was hiding too. Hani asked them both again to leave him and run on home but they both refused. They asked him which of his wounds hurt him most and he said the arrow in his back hurt him the worst. So they thought they would pull this arrow out, but it was stuck fast in the bone. They tried it, but the shaft came off from the point. Then it was even harder to pull out. So they both tried their teeth on it and finally they pulled it out. One of these men was asked to scout ahead and the other to scout behind. So each man was supposed to be about one-fourth mile from the wounded man.

They were going very slowly. Finally they went down into another valley. It was about sunrise. As they were going along Hani saw a rabbit, a little cottontail on the side of the trail, and he wanted to shoot this rabbit because he said he was hungry and needed something to eat. Well, the other man said not to kill the rabbit. He said, "You belong to the Rabbit Clan and you can't kill that rabbit. It might bring you luck if left alive. It might bring us both luck." So he said, "Let the rabbit live."

They thought of a spring around the point, for they were both tired and thirsty. Instead of scouting ahead, the third man, Tochi, had run home. When they got to the spring Mai-yaro would not let the wounded boy have a big drink, thinking that his stomach was injured. When they got kind of cooled off, Mai-yaro thought he would look back over the hill and see if the enemy was following. Before he left, he told the wounded man not to drink any more, for if his stomach was injured badly it would not hold water. But just as soon as he left Hani took a big drink and he felt much better.

Well, Mai-yaro went over the hill and as he looked down on the trail he saw a Navajo walking back and forth over the trail. He watched this Navajo for quite a while and he saw that he was very much discouraged. Well, finally, the Navajo turned back, so Mai-yaro went back to the spring and when he got there Hani told him he had had a big drink and felt better and he asked to have some more.

Then they both started back for the trail. This man, Mai-yaro, said he would go back to the trail and see what the Navajo was doing. When he got where they had seen the rabbit he found that the rabbit was gone. So he investigated there and found that the rabbit had gone over their tracks three times, So the rabbit had disappointed the Navajo who thought the men had passed him in the night long before daylight.

It was about the middle of the day, and it was hot, so they got in among some rocks. Hani was pretty well tired out and he said he would like to lie down for awhile and cool himself off. So he did lie down under one of the rocks and fell right asleep and the other man kept awake. Well, this man on the watch would close his eyes every little while and as he was doing this, he saw the shadow of a little bird on top of a rock. It was a little rock sparrow and it was very much excited about something. The man thought this was a warning to them, so they got right up and started on.

As they were going along it began to show signs that it was going to rain. Clouds were coming up. When it did cloud up they felt very much better, for they were cooled off. Then it started to rain. They thought they would not stop for shelter, but kept right on going while it rained. Finally, it poured down on them and there was a regular cloudburst. It rained so hard on them that it washed all the blood off Hani. He said that he felt very much better, so Mai-yaro asked him to try himself out on a trot.

The man asked him if he felt his wounds hurting him and he said, "No." Then he asked him to go a little faster, and then he asked him again how he felt. Hani said that he felt all right, so Mai-yaro asked him to run as fast as he could. Then he asked him again if the wounds hurt him. Hani said, "No," and thought that he was well, so Mai-yaro said, "Let's go then."

Now when Tochi reached Walpi and told the people what had happened, Hani's mother heard that he had been wounded badly and might die, so she wrapped up some piki and some sweet corn meal and she started out to look for him, all by herself. Now this was a very brave thing for a Hopi woman to do. She thought that she might find him dead somewhere and if she did she would roll his body under a ledge of rock or a bank of earth and cover him up with heavy stones and she would leave the piki and the sweet corn meal there for him.

But near the head of Jeddito Canyon she saw two men coming and then she recognized them for it was her boy Hani and Mai-yaro with him. And when they met they could not help but cry for joy. They hurried on home from there and when they came to the edge of the mesa south of Walpi, they saw clouds of dust in the valley coming toward them. They wondered what it was and thought it was an attack on the mesa. So they said to themselves, if there was an attack they would go on and meet the Navajo. So they went on and were met halfway and they found that this was a war party sent out to help them. When they met the whole party hurried back to the mesa and there at the foot of the mesa the whole village was crying for they found that only six men were saved out of the party that went to Fort Defiance.

Hani chose his godfather at the foot of the mesa, and of course it was Mai-yaro who was the first one to find him wounded, so instead of going to his own house he went with this man to be washed up and cared for the next day. When this was done he fasted four days. On the fourth day he was given his new name, "Hani." From then on he always had in mind to get even with the Navajos in that part of the country, and so he did, for later he led war parties to that country often and brought back a scalp every time. He was considered one of the greatest and bravest men of the Walpi villages.

CHAPTER XII
HOW SOME HOPIS RESISTED SENDING THEIR CHILDREN TO SCHOOL AND THE TROUBLE THAT RESULTED

OUT this time the agency was established at Keams Canyon and of course the Hopis knew that this meant peace. So all the chiefs from every village went there and told the white man that they were his friends and brothers and they told him that they would like to be protected by him from all their other enemies. For this reason they thought the agent ought to settle all their troubles which they had been having right along.

Later, a school was established there and all the Hopis were willing to send their children to school. Everything was going all right until they had an initiation ceremony (*Wuwuchime*) at Shung-opovi and the young men at old Shung-opovi and Shipaulovi were to be initiated. So they were not sent back to school that year and of course, at that time, these ceremonies were not very well understood by the white man, so the agent sent out policemen (two First Mesa men and three Navajos) to fetch the young boys. When they got to Shipaulovi they found the young men in the kiva and they asked the chief to give them up so that they could take them back to school. The chief said he would not let them go until the ceremony was over and he told them that he would be quite willing to let them go then. But the policemen insisted that they must take them at once because they had orders to bring them in. But the chief just flatly refused.

So the policeman said that they would take the chief instead. He said he would be willing to go with them after he had seen his friend, the missionary. So he went off and as he was leaving, he asked the policeman to stay on top of the mesa and wait for him until he came back.

He started off for the Sunlight Mission by way of Mishongnovi. The policemen thought that he was going to fool them, so they followed him and caught up with him as he was going around the village. They took hold of him and dragged him off the mesa, so he did not get to see the chief at Mishongnovi either. He intended that they would both go down to the mission to see what information they could get from the missionary. In both villages there was much excitement and all the people were on the housetops as they were very much troubled to see the chief dragged off the mesa by the policemen.

The three sons of the chief ran out after them and they caught up with them just as they were at the bottom of the mesa, and, of course, they could not help but fight these men to defend their father. But finally they all got to the mission. When they got there, the missionary took the side of the chief and told the policeman to let him go. Then he wrote a letter to the agent asking him to let him know what orders he had given these policemen to come out to do. While he was writing this letter the chief asked him to put in this message to the agent, that he was through with the school and that he would not be his friend any more. And he said that he was a friend of the missionary only and that he would do anything for him. So he said that if the agent were man enough he could come and get his scalp. Then he said, "I am the man, Tawahonganiwa. If you ever want to come out, get no one else but Tawahonganiwa. I am not your friend."

When this was written the missionary enclosed the letter in an envelope and gave it to the policeman to take into the agency. This was how the two factions and all the trouble over sending the children to school was started among the Hopi.

From then on, Chief Tawahonganiwa had many followers in both Mishongnovi and Shipaulovi and every now and then he would hold a council with his fellowmen. Then later, many people of the other villages took up his side, excepting First Mesa.

When they split those that wanted to go to school went right on; but the Chief's relatives had to take his side and held their children back. This was about 1888 or 1889. Every once in a while the agent would send out the policemen. If they were expecting them, the parents would have to go out early with their children to the hiding places under the cliffs. Not finding any children, the policemen would go back.

Finally the policemen thought of the scheme of coming into the villages at night. In that way they got quite a few children and they took them off to Keams Canyon to boarding school. Of course, this was very unpleasant for the Hopis, for they never before had parted with any of their children. So the Chief at Mishongnovi thought that it would be best to let their children be sent to school with their own consent.

About this time, the army (a troop of negro soldiers) was sent out to the Hopi villages to see if they could make the old chief at Shipaulovi change his mind about sending his children to school. They did not stop at Shipaulovi very long, but went on to Oraibi where there were more people. There they were met by the chief, Lololama, and he was very friendly to them and said he was willing to send his children to school. He wanted to take advantage of what the outcome would be of sending the children to school. After he made this agreement Youkioma jumped on him and they quarreled. This was the first time that Lololama had found out that Youkioma was the leader of this other faction. But Lololama, being the chief, said that the children who were old enough to go to the Keams Canyon School could be taken. Now from then on these two men were against each other and each man wanted to see how many followers he could have. These hostile leaders would have meetings at every other village ever so often and they would lecture to the people, telling them that the ones who were sending their children to school would be in worse trouble because the Bahana who established the school was not their true brother who had come up from the underworld with them. If he was, he would have shown the Hopis his written tradition to compare with their tradition. So this faction felt that they would rather wait for their Bahana brother to come with this written story of their ancestors.

This sort of trouble got very bad among the people themselves and the leaders of each faction of course, were working against one another to see who would have the most followers. On account of many good useful things, like tools, such as axes and hoes, clothing and sugar and coffee some of the hostile faction people began falling off, thinking that the idea of being a hostile was just the idea of preventing the people from having these things. Finally it got so there were very few hostiles left at Shipaulovi and Mishongnovi, but there were quite a number at Shung-opovi, so the ones at Shipaulovi moved over to Shung-opovi. This move occurred in 1899.

CHAPTER XIII
HOW HOTEVILLA AND BAKABI WERE FOUNDED

WHILE the Shipaulovi hostiles were living over at Shung-opovi they were very much stronger against the school. The agent would send out policemen every once in awhile to try to get their leader, Tawahonganiwa. Of course those policemen did not have much authority, so they could not take him. He would put up a big fight and his sons were the ones who would do the fighting. These policemen were mostly Navajos.

The move to Shung-opovi occurred after the people had the smallpox and the government was fumigating all the villages. The government people were trying to get these hostiles over to the Toreva school to give them a good cleaning up, so they could give them clean clothes and burn up what they were wearing, but these hostiles did not want to go there, because they did not want to put on what the government would issue to them. So finally the Agent had to send out a regiment, composed of colored soldiers from Fort Wingate. When these soldiers arrived the hostile women made up a lot of piki and took it over to the soldiers to feed them, thinking that the soldiers might recognize them when they came up to the Mesa. The next morning the captain sent over a soldier to warn the people that they must be ready to come right along, otherwise there would be some shooting. But Tawahonganiwa refused to do as he was bid and said he would not go. He said if they wanted to take him they would have to kill him, so he called all his followers, women and all, to one house. Whoever was an officer or priest of some kind in some of the societies would take in an image or emblem to put in the house. One of these families happened to have the image of the war god, Piakonghoya. This little image was put up by the door, for they thought he might have some power to help them. When the soldiers came up on top of the mesa they were lined up about one-fourth mile outside the village and from there the captain sent in policemen to ask these hostiles to surrender. They were asked four times, but they refused every time. So the captain thought it was time to march up. When they got there, they surrounded this house and the captain went to the house himself and asked them if they were ready to surrender and they refused again, so then it was time to take them by force, so he gave orders to the soldiers to take picks and dig around the walls and on the housetops. There must have been about seventy-five or a hundred people in this house. Just as soon as the picks were seen coming through the roofs they all started to run out and as they did this they were taken hold of by the soldiers. The leader was the last one to come out and just as soon as he was outside the door he was grabbed by the soldiers and his five sons piled up on them and the fight began.

They fought there for quite awhile. All the hostile people were fighting with the soldiers, hand to hand. Finally the old chief was knocked out and all the sons had their hands tied up behind their backs. Their father was strapped on to a horse and they were all taken to the Toreva School and there they were given baths and clean clothes and what clothes they had on were taken away and burned.

The smallpox epidemic had not yet spread to Oraibi which was well guarded so that nobody could go there. (The agent's name was Migle and the man in charge of the fumigation, etc., was Sam Shoemaker.) Most of the leading men of the hostiles were put under arrest and taken to Keams Canyon the next day and then on to Fort Defiance. They were kept at Fort Defiance for about 90 days and after that they were sent home, on their agreement that they would behave, themselves. When they got home they turned back and were just as hostile as before they were taken. They said the white man was a fool to let them go, for he was just fooled by them.

They didn't make very much trouble from then on, though their ideas against the schools were just as strong as ever and the two factions would be saying all kinds of things about one another. They were quiet from then on, but, of course, many of their followers began to fall away from the hostiles because they thought that the chief at Shung-opovi had not recognized them, so some of these people went back to Shipaulovi.

The trouble started again in the year 1906, and this was between the same two factions. It started in Shung-opovi and this was during the time of the Bean Dance. The hostiles did not plant their crop of beans with the others and eight days later they came into the kiva to plant their crop. One kiva was divided up—part hostiles and part friendlies. The night of the dance they asked these hostiles to get their plants out of the kiva because some young children who were not initiated into the Kachina ceremony would see the plants. But these men refused to take their plants away because it was against their law to take plants out of the kiva before their time. So in order to have a dance they brought in several wedding robes so as to hide the plants from the children. From then on those people were always fighting one another. So again the hostile leader decided to leave. From there Tawahonganiwa and twenty-five to thirty men and women moved to Oraibi. By this time Lololama was dead and his nephew, Tewaquoptiwa was then chief of Oraibi, but Youkioma was stronger at this time. When they got to the mesa top at Oraibi, Youkioma's men met them. These men sprinkled sacred cornmeal on the path that the Shung-opovi people followed to the village. Of course this was not the proper thing to do, for Youkioma was usurping the chief's function and Chief Tewaquoptiwa did not like it.

The leading men from both sides held council every once in a while trying to see what must be done with these people who were being taken in by Youkioma, and Youkioma always said that he had as much right to do this as the chief. It was his "theory" that he was going to follow out what his great-uncles had taught him of their traditions. This tradition told him that he was to destroy Oraibi or be destroyed himself. He belonged to the Fire or Masauwu Clan. This gave him the idea that his clan ancestor had the power to do almost anything. This clan has the idea that Masauwu can hypnotize people, so he always had said that if any expedition is sent against him all he has to do is to take out a handful of ashes and blow them on the army and they would fall to pieces. Chief Tewaquoptiwa wanted to send these people back to Shungopovi, but Youkioma, of course, was standing up for them and if Tewaquoptiwa wanted to move them he would have had to move him too. He said that he had already had a site picked out somewhere in the north called Kawishtima (a ruin in a canyon near Navajo Mountain).

As long as he had this site already picked out Tewaquoptiwa wanted to send him there, but Tewaquoptiwa was in doubt that Youkioma would go there. Finally this trouble got so bad that if the two parties should happen to meet out in the street they would start an argument and whoever was passing would stop too and it would get worse and worse.

The people of Oraibi got so that they were very much troubled and impatient and at last they decided to move them out. Right at this time they were having a Snake Dance and Youkioma insisted he would like to be moved away on this day, but Tewaquoptiwa refused to do anything with him on that day because of the ceremony, for he did not want to trouble this religious party. So he set the day for the fourth day after the dance. From the many arguments that all the people had had in the streets both sides had the idea that there would be a fight, so they tried to collect as many weapons as possible-bows and arrows and guns, and to get them ready. Come to find out, Tewaquoptiwa did not have enough men and the hostiles were about three or four times as many as his people. So he called on the Moenkopi people for help and all the other villages of Second Mesa.

The night before the fight both parties stayed up all night for their luck, because this was rather a ceremony. They smoked all night long. When morning came Tewaquoptiwa went to the house where the hostile party was and asked them if they were ready for the day and were willing to put up a fight against his people. He also asked them if any of them would be ready to surrender and follow him. But none would surrender, because of the good sayings of Youkioma and how he was going to take them to a prosperous land.

During these hours of the morning, the men on both sides had rather a creepy feeling about what was going to be the outcome, and the men out in the streets gathered here and there listening to the many arguments. The Oraibi chief made his request four times of the hostile party. Each time he asked them if they would be willing to take the step and leave of their own free will, and that if they would, they would not be bothered or hunted. But each time Youkioma said he would have to be forced to move out. Come to find out, Tewaquoptiwa was a little afraid and he did not have nerve enough to go in and put Youkioma out of the house. So one of the men on the Chief's side was rather tired of all this foolishness that they were going through, so he called the chief, Tewaquoptiwa, a coward and jumped into the house. When he did that the rest of the men followed. When they got in there they got hold of Youkioma and just slung him out of the door. When he landed outside another party picked him up. By this time the men in the street had formed a double line and the men in the house just kept throwing men out and passing them down the line. It seemed as though they were handed out and as if they were unloading sacks of flour or watermelons and passing them on down the line. Every now and then someone would put up a fight but he was pretty well beaten. Now this was kept up until they had emptied the house. When Tewaquoptiwa's men were through they went through the village and got all the hostile women out and drove them to the outside of the village.

On that morning the missionaries had come up and they made the people on both sides give up their weapons and they took them all away. They said it would not be fair for them to have weapons, but they could fight all they wanted, hand to hand.

They passed all the hostiles out of the village and it was something awful on both sides—women and children crying. It might be sisters, it might be brothers, mothers and daughters that were separated. Just about this time one old man, a hostile, came up from his field. The day before he had baked some corn in his ground oven and he had eight burros loaded with sacks of corn, each sack holding about 100 to 150 pounds. When he came to his house no one was at home. Then someone came and drove him out with his burros and when he got out there the hostile people ripped up the sacks and helped themselves. Again Chief Tewaquoptiwa went out and asked them if they were ready to move on. Youkioma said he would not move unless Tewaquoptiwa could push him across the line which he had drawn on the flat rock of the mesa top. So here they had to put up another fight again, to put Youkioma across the line. When the chief was ready to go against them, the hostile men gathered about Youkioma, intending to hold him so that the other side could not move him across the line. Then the fight began, one party pushing toward the village and another pushing away from the village.

Tewaquoptiwa had about one hundred men and Youkioma about two hundred. There they pushed back and forth for two hours and a half. When they got out of breath they stopped and then began again. Every once in awhile the pressure would be so great that old Youkioma would rise up in the air. Being quite a bunch of men they were hard to move.

One of the men from Shung-opovi, a friendly who was looking on from a housetop, could not stand it, he was so excited, and seeing one of his relations in the crowd, he dragged him away and threw him up in the air and did it again and again.

Tewaquoptiwa's men found they could pull away their relatives too. They did not like to fight other clans and all this time they had a hard feeling against their relatives who had gone over to the hostiles. By doing this they reduced the hostiles quite a bit, but no one knew why Youkioma was in the midst of the crowd. He must have had some object on either side that he was looking out for. Just as soon as he was pushed over the line, he said, "It is done, I have passed my mark," and all at once they dropped him. When this was done Chief Tewaquoptiwa asked them if they would like to take anything along, food and bedding. He told them they could go back to the village for it, so they did. The men went back and got their bedding and the women got piki and food. All this time the children were crying for something to eat and they were very thirsty. Well, that evening the whole village was like a disturbed anthill. People were everywhere, coming and going and people from other villages were there to see what was going on. You would see a woman with a bundle on her back crying and other people would be making fun of them because they were crying.

Just about sundown they were already to move on-all their burros were loaded and they were pretty well packed themselves. Youkioma took the lead and off they went to the north. They got to Hotevilla just about dark and there they made camp.

CHAPTER XIV
YOUKIOMA

ON THE next day at this place they started to clear out under the trees and cut out the lower limbs so they could have shade. But of course, some of those men who did not really know what this was all about argued here and there and some thought they should go back to Oraibi and make an attack on the Oraibi chief. Somehow the chief of Oraibi heard about this, but by that time the men from Moenkopi had gone back home and he knew he could not very well protect his town if they all came back. So he sent two men out, one to Moenkopi and one to Second Mesa to call for help. But, of course, all the men were out in the field by this time and it was quite late at night when these men heard about it. But anyway they thought they would go there to see if the people had come back to make this attack. When they got there all the men were at the chief's house. There he was, feeding the men on some peaches and melons which were taken from the orchards and fields of the people he had sent away. All night long some of the men were out along the edges of the mesa watching, for they did not know which way the people would come to make the attack. They had guns and what other weapons they could find.

All night long the men took turns going about the edge of the mesa, about six at the north and all at a good running distance from each other, but no enemy had shown up by daybreak so they felt quite sure they were safe.

From then on, all the mesa was pretty well guarded during both day and night and every man coming in from Hotevilla for this things was searched before he was allowed to go into the village.

During all this time the government hadn't interfered until about a month after. Of course, some of the children who had been going to school had gone to Hotevilla and when they tried to get them to go to school, trouble began again. The Hotevilla people would not let their children go back to school, saying they did not have to send the children because they had left the place from which they had been going to school. Every time when the policemen were sent all the people would come out and they could do nothing and had to go back without the children.

About the middle of October of that year, 1906, the army was sent out. They did not go clear to Hotevilla, but made camp at Lower Oraibi. About a couple of days after this they sent word to Hotevilla that they had come to see what the trouble was and if they could help them settle it, they would. Well, Chief Youkioma sent word back to the captain that he did not need his help. The trouble was already settled, but he had moved away from Oraibi. He also said he expected to live in peace, if there was going to be any.

Then the captain sent word back again, asking him if he would mind telling him what had caused him to move. And again Youkioma sent word back to the captain saying he would not tell him unless Chief Tewaquoptiwa would tell him first what this was all about. Then the captain sent for the Oraibi chief. Being friendly to the white man he went right down with his interpreter, and when he got there the captain asked him why he had sent those people away. He said that he had been having so much trouble with them and that they could not get along together in the same village. So the captain asked the chief why it was, and he said it was on account of their not being friendly to the white men and because they did not want to send their children to school. Before the white men had built schools, everything had been going all right. So he said that it was his fault that the trouble had begun some years ago.

The captain said that this chief should not have sent those people away. Since the white men caused the trouble it was for the white man to handle it. The chief thought that he was doing something for his friend, the white man, but he was told that it was wrong to send those people away where there was no shelter, so that he would have to bring them back or serve a term in prison. He said he did not expect to serve a term in prison, for he thought that he was doing something for the government. He told the captain that it was his "theory" that he move the hostile chief out of the village. Youkioma knew that these things were going to happen too and it had happened so. He said that if it had not been for the missionaries who interfered they would have killed each other, Tewaquoptiwa and Youkioma.

The captain said he still had a chance to kill Youkioma, but Tewaquoptiwa said it was all over now. The captain said that that was not the place where the people should settle and he said that Tewaquoptiwa still had a chance to kill Youkioma if he wanted to. He also said that the next morning at sunrise he would give him a chance to do this. He would not let Tewaquoptiwa go home that night and all this time Tewaquoptiwa did not know that he was under arrest.

In the meantime, after nightfall, the captain sent soldiers up in the draw by Bakabi and twenty-five or thirty Navajos on police duty below Hotevilla Spring. In the meantime word was sent to Youkioma that he must be ready to be shot at sunrise the next morning. So about dawn the captain, Tewaquoptiwa, and two Hopi policemen, one Oraibi, and one Second Mesa policeman, and a guard came to Hotevilla and at the sand dune the captain gave automatics to Tewaquoptiwa and to his interpreter.

Youkioma was waiting for them on the top of a sand dune. They slowly moved up on the hostile chief who stood on the top of the sand dune, waiting for his time to come. He was all by himself, but behind the sand dune his men were hidden with all the weapons they could find.

They intended to kill Tewaquoptiwa if Tewaquoptiwa killed Youkioma.

When the sun came up the captain told Tewaquoptiwa to walk up to Youkioma, but he refused to move. He was asked four times by the captain, but he was so scared that he could not talk. His jaw was shaking too fast. Since the Oraibi chief could not move the captain asked Youkioma to come over. So he came, not a bit frightened, and the captain asked him if he was ready to be shot. He said he was, for this was the sad day that would be his end. The captain asked Tewaquoptiwa if he was ready to do his duty that he was expected to do, but he would not speak. He was so weak from fright that he could hardly stand up. Then the captain asked Youkioma if he would want to take the gun away from his rival and do away with him, but Youkioma said no, that that was not his "theory". His theory was only that he would get his followers away from the old chief, to a better place. He said the Oraibi chief did not understand his "theory," and that he was all wrong. However, even if he was wrong and had always had in mind about doing away with him, he was willing to let him do it. He was willing to die for his people.

So the captain turned back to Tewaquoptiwa and asked him if he would do it now, since his rival had voluntarily given himself up and was willing to die for his people. The chief said that he would not do it because he said Youkioma must be right and that he himself had made a mistake in thinking of doing away with him. Then Tewaquoptiwa asked the captain what he would do with him if he had killed the old man (Youkioma).

The captain said that Tewaquoptiwa was mistaken in sending the people away like that and he answered that if it was not for this "theory" he would never have done it. Then the captain asked him where he got this "theory" and he said he got it all from his great-uncles. It had been handed down for a good many years and he was chosen to carry this out. The captain said he was sorry to say that his great-uncles must have been pretty mean to have made such a theory and to give it to him to carry it out; that he had been misled and he was not doing anything right for his people or for the government. So the captain told him that this was not only a mistake but a big crime that he had done, to send the people away without anything to eat. Again he asked him if he realized how bad the situation was—that the children were crying for something to eat. Well, the chief said he did realize it then, but it was too late. But the captain said it was not too late; that the houses the people had left were still full of corn and he warned him not to interfere with any men going to Oraibi for food. Tewaquoptiwa agreed to all of this and then he asked the captain if that was all for him but the captain said no. So right there he told him that he was under arrest and that he was going to be taken away some place to serve his term in prison. Tewaquoptiwa asked the captain if he really meant it and he said yes, he had to do it. The chief turned to the captain and asked for mercy and the captain said there was nothing he could do. Then the chief cried like a child and again he asked the captain if he could spend a few days with his people. The captain said that he did not allow his prisoners to spend time with their people but they had to stay around his camp.

The chief said if he was allowed to stay with his people he would show the captain all the different ceremonies that he could perform. He said he would show the captain his most beautiful dance which his people would dance for him. The captain saw he had a chance to see these beautiful dances, so he told the chief not to spend too much time getting the dance up as his time was limited. From then on Tewaquoptiwa got his people to practice a butterfly dance.

During this time the captain returned to Youkioma. He sent for the old man. Youkioma gathered his best men and went to see the captain. When he arrived the captain asked him if he was ready to surrender and send the children to school. The chief said he was not ready for that yet, because he was still expecting to go on to the chosen site for his new village. Again the captain asked him if he would send the children to school so that they would be well taken care of at school and then the others could go on, but Youkioma said no, that he was the father of all and he would leave none behind. The captain said that he must leave them behind if he did not surrender. The chief said that even if he had to serve another term in prison he would go on when he got out again, so the captain said he would send him back home to think it over. The chief agreed to think it over, but said he could not change his mind. When he got home that night and those that went with him broke the news to the people, that was all that they talked of that night. Some had the idea that he would surrender to the captain so as to relieve the trouble of the people.

Now in the next few days there was another division among the people.

After a few days Chief Youkioma was called again and all the men followed him to Kiakochomovi. The captain asked him again if he had changed his mind or decided to surrender. He said, "No." Then the captain asked all the men who came down with Youkioma if they were all with him and would they not surrender. All who were strong with the old chief were asked to step to his side. Before anybody had moved Kiwanimptiwa stepped up and said that he was ready to surrender and that there were some others that would follow him. The captain asked, "Who are they?" Chief Youkioma was put to one side and Chief Kiwanimptiwa on the other side, and the captain said, "Take your choice." Of course there was then a big argument. Some were very undecided because they did not know who was right, but most of them went over to Youkioma's side. After this was done the captain told them that all who went on Youkioma's side were under arrest and would be taken away. All that went on Kiwanimptiwa's side were to be sent back to try to make up with Tewaquoptiwa at Oraibi, so that they could return to their homes.

Youkioma's followers all stayed down at the camp and Kiwanimptiwa's followers went back to Hotevilla. When they came back, they told their families that they had shaken hands with the captain. The next day Kiwanimptiwa went back to Oraibi to see Tewaquoptiwa. When he got there he told the chief what had happened when he had visited the captain and the chief said that he would let them come back but he would like to see all the men who had shaken hands with the captain.

That same night these men went back to Oraibi to have a council with the chief. At this council the chief told them they could come back if they would be willing to send their children to school like the rest of the people and they said they would agree to this.

In a few days they came back to Oraibi with their families and shortly after that the Butterfly Dance took place. On that day all the soldiers were up in the village to see the dance.

The next day after the dance, the police and some soldiers went to Hotevilla to get the children of school age, to send them to Keams Canyon to the school, and on that same afternoon the army broke camp and left Oraibi with their prisoners, Youkioma and his men, and the children. When they arrived at Keams Canyon the captain asked the agent to look the prisoners over and point out the men who had made trouble for him before. On looking them over he picked out Chief Youkioma first. Next was Chief Tewahonganewa of Shipaulovi and all his followers.

So the two chiefs had something like fifteen men picked out with them. Besides these, eleven men were picked out to be sent to Carlysle School (1. Archie Quamala, 2. Glen Chestiwa, 3. Andrew Humiquoptiwa, 4. Joshua Humiyistiwa, 5. Washington Tala-umptiwa, 6. Louis Tiwanima, all from Shung-opovi; 7. William Strong, 8. Albert Tawaventiwa, 9. Quoits-hoeoma, 10. Arthur Ponyaquoptiwa, 11. Tewanimptiwa, from Hotevilla.)

The two chiefs, Youkioma and Tawahonganiwa, with their fifteen followers and the boys were taken on to Fort Wingate. The rest of the men (about one hundred) were left at Keams Canyon.

From Fort Wingate these prisoners were sent to Florence penitentiary. The other eleven men, who were all married, were sent to Carlysle School. Three of the boys, Archie, Andrew, and Louis, had left their wives at Shung-opovi when they went to Oraibi.

When the soldiers went away, Chief Tewaquoptiwa thought that the captain had forgotten him, but when the captain arrived at Fort Wingate he wrote to him and he had to go away, either to Riverside or Phoenix. This was a month after the others had left.

About this time, Tewaquoptiwa had insulted some of the women who came back from Hotevilla and of course Kiwanimptiwa could not stand for this, so he called together all his followers, men, women, and all, about fifteen or so families and when he got them together, he asked them how long this had been going on, and they said, ever since they had come back. They said that the chief had always said to them that if they wanted to stay in that village they had to do as the Oraibi people asked them to, whether they wanted to or not. After hearing all this from the women folk Kiwanimptiwa went and called Chief Tewaquoptiwa in and when he did bring him in he said that the women had told him what he had been doing. Tewaquoptiwa said it was not so, but the women stood right up and told him it was so and there was no use f or him to try to hide it. Then, of course, after that there was an argument. Finally, the chief told them that they did not have to stay there, but could go any place they wanted to—to Hotevilla or any place else.

They knew that after having left Hotevilla they could not go back there, so the next day, Kiwanimptiwa went out to look for a site. First he went to a spring, Meumeushva, below Hukovi. Then he came back upon the mesa and went to Bakabi. Finding that place with plenty of water and wood he decided to take his people there, so when he came back he told his people they were to move the next day.

The next morning all their burros were packed up with their stuff. (This was almost the middle of October.) When they got there, the Hotevilla people hearing of it, did not like it because after splitting away from them they were coming back to a place so near them.

Of course, this being the fall, the weather was getting cold and the best they could do was to find a little shelter along the edge of the cliff and a few of them were under the ledge. Of course in both places, Bakabi and Hotevilla, the people were busy trying to put up houses of some kind. In Hotevilla the women had to do all the work, for there were just a few old grandfathers left to help them.

Mr. Lemon, the agent, after hearing about this trouble again at Oraibi, came right out and sent Tewaquoptiwa to Riverside. They just keep him there and he did a little work. After sending him to Riverside School the agent went back to Hotevilla and picked out all the Shung-opovi families and sent them back to their homes.

Kiwanimptiwa thought he should have help from the government, since he had shaken hands with the captain and made friends with the white man, so he went to the agency to ask for help. When he got there he told the agent he would like him to see if he could help him out and the agent asked him in what way. The chief said he would like some lumber for doors and windows. Well, the agent thought it was rather wise of him to call on him for help, so he ordered some ready-made doors and windows. But these windows and doors did not come until the spring, about April. Of course, at both places, the people had a hard time during the cold weather. They had built little shelter places of stone with what cedar beams they could get, and they got through the winter pretty well and not many people died. The Hotevilla people had taken some of their beans from Oraibi and with burros they had dragged them over. The women went back and forth every day and carried their doors and their metates. The Oraibi people had taken all their string-beans and jerky.

The men at Keams Canyon were set free about April. They were let out in time to plant their crops. The men sent to Florence were kept there about a year and a half. Along with these men was one man they thought was a witch, Quoitsventiwa, and he would slip out of his cell (mysteriously) once in a while. Once he got out and ran away from the prison, but they caught him again, up in the mountains. While they were there, of course, their leaders—Youkioma and Tawahonganiwa,—always would refuse to answer whenever the warden or superintendent would ask them if they were ready to surrender and be sent back home. The others were quite young, and having left their families behind they wanted to go home, and so of course they were always having trouble among themselves.

Finally, the two chiefs surrendered and were sent home, but after they came home they had a feeling that they were not respected—especially those that came from Shung-opovi.

Everything went well for about a year at Hotevilla and Shung-opovi. Then the children came home from school in the summer. At Hotevilla houses had been built by this time. When the school opened in the fall, the people, would not let the children return. The policemen went out but returned without the children. Again the army was called in. One company arrived and went to Hotevilla, caught the children, and then went on to Shung-opovi. At Shung-opovi the hostile group ref used to send their children and hid them. After that the children of the hostile group were not allowed to go home in the summer.

From then on, everything went well. The old chief at Shipaulovi, Tawahonganiwa died at Shung-opovi about 1920, and his followers all mixed with the other people. When Tawahonganiwa became hostile Sikia-litstiwa became chief of Shipaulovi.

Later Youkioma was again arrested and taken to California because he refused to have the sheep dipped—he thought it was bad for the sheep and he thought the dipping caused the scab. He was arrested and sent to Keams Canyon. There were about fifteen men from Hotevilla, mostly sheep owners.

When his time came to be released, Mr. Daniels, the agent, called him into the office at Keams Canyon and asked him if he was ready to go back home.

The old chief said, "Yes, but I will never change my heart and the idea of making a friend of the white man. I am old now and I am not able to serve any more terms in prison. As far as my "theory" is concerned, I think that I have carried it out well for my great-uncles who gave me this theory to carry out. When I go back to my people I will ask them or my relatives if they will carry this on, but I think that they will not do as well as I have done, because they will be afraid. They will not be men enough to do it, but whoever does step in and take my place in prison I think will be Chief Tewaquoptiwa, because he will carry on and make trouble for you as he did for me, and if he ever does serve a prison term, I wish to see if he is as brave as I am and will stand as much as I have stood to this day. So I am through. From now on I hope to live in peace and die in peace." He did.

HOW THE CROW CLAN BECAME ALSO THE KACHINA CLAN

ORIGINALLY, the home of the Crow Clan was somewhere in the forest at the foot of the San Francisco Peaks. There were seven families and they were a dark people. Now, often in the night they would hear something moving about far away in the woods, making a strange noise and they wondered who it was. The leader of the village wanted to find out about this strange sound, for he knew that no animal made that kind of a sound, like a deep growling (for in those days this person wore a bell made out of mountain sheep horn, which rattled and could be heard a long distance).

So finally the Chief said he would send out a few boys who were good runners, to spy around and see who this person could be. And so one night he did send out seven of them into the forest. They wandered around and finally, away in the distance, they heard the strange noise, far up at the top of the peaks, coming down from point to point and they were frightened. The noise came on, passed them and came down on the flat and traveled on toward the village. The boys saw that it was someone, but they feared that it might be a man of great power who would kill them and they did not try to catch him.

So this man, or whoever it was, came close to the village again and finally went away up the mountain. Now someone said to the Chief that this person, whoever he was, that came from the peaks must surely live up there, so that it would be well for him to hold the ceremony of the "Paho making." So he called the High Priest and had him make prayer offerings.

After thinking it over the Chief decided to send one of his nephews with the offerings so that. if he found anyone on the peaks and harm should come to the youth, as he was a relative, there would be no trouble.

So he called his nephew and gave him the pahos and told him to go up the mountain and give the pahos to anyone that he might find there. Now they got the youth ready next morning and painted him in reddish clay and tied a prayer plume on his head. Every man who had made a prayer offering went and placed it on a white buckskin and after they were all delivered there, they wrapped them up nicely and gave them to the youth together with a sack of sacred corn meal. Before the boy started, the Chief told him that if there were supernatural beings up there, to tell them that the Chief had sent them a message. He would like to ask if they were gods or other spirits and if they were, he would like to communicate with them. If they were spirits, then the people would worship them and accept their advice, because he knows himself, who must have control of the weather.

So the youth started out, but before he commenced to ascend he came upon the old Spider Woman. The Spider Woman spoke to the youth, but he could not see her anywhere, so she peeped a little more out of her hole and she said to him, "Come in."

But the youth looked down and said sadly, "How can I, the hole is too small." So she said, "Stick in your foot and wriggle it around a little." He did as she told him and the hole grew larger and he went down into her pithouse.

The wise old Spider Woman said to the youth, "My poor boy, I am sorry for you. You have been sent up there on a difficult journey and I am afraid you are going to have a very hard time. You will have to do the best you can. There are four dangerous places that you must pass, guarded by 'terrible beings.' I will give you a charm which will make these creatures harmless and you can pass in safety." She handed him the root of a plant and told him how to use it. Whenever he came up one of these guards (it might be a mountain lion, a bear, or a terrible snake) the Spider Woman charged him to chew the magic root and spray it out upon the creature and he would immediately become mild and gentle. Then the old woman gave him a little fluffy feather and directed him how to use it, and told him which way to go.

So the youth started out and traveled upward about three quarters of the way when he discerned a very faint trail and it was difficult to follow. All at once he thought of the little feather that the old Spider Woman had given him and how she had told him that it would go before him and show the way. So the youth took out his feather and let it go and it rose in the air and flew along before him, very slowly, so that he could easily follow it.

No sooner had he started than he came to the first guard. A great mountain lion lay across his way and when he saw the boy he growled in his throat and crouched ready to spring upon him. The youth was frightened but he remembered the old Spider Woman's words and he quickly chewed the magic root and sprayed it out upon the angry lion and at once the beast lay down and it seemed as if he had never noticed the boy.

Now all this time, the little feather danced along ahead of the youth and presently they came to the second guard, a giant grizzly bear. Of course you know, this animal is very fierce and the boy was even more afraid than he had been of the mountain lion, but he quickly chewed more of the magic medicine and sprayed it out over the bear and at once he became quiet and the youth passed on.

Finally, with the feather going before he reached the top of the mountains and there he found a kiva. This kiva was guarded by two snakes, a great rattler, and a small rattler more deadly than the first. When they saw him approaching they coiled ready to strike and the boy stopped a long way off and felt very much discouraged and he forgot about his magic medicine. But the little feather had gone on ahead and stopped over the two snakes on top of the kiva. Now the snakes looked at the little feather and then at the youth and they thought that the feather was the boy's spirit. Then the youth remembered his charm and sprayed the snakes and they quieted down, uncoiled and crawled away from the entrance to the kiva.

The feather entered the kiva and the youth followed. One lone man was sitting by the fire-place and he did not notice the youth. So the boy stood by the ladder and waited and presently the man saw him and asked him to be seated. The youth had a pipe which he filled with tobacco, lit it at the fire and passed it to the old man, who took four puffs and all the tobacco was used up; but the odor of the tobacco filled the room. Now he asked the youth where he had come from and who had sent him and the youth said that his uncle, the Chief, had sent him to find out who it was that visited the village and returned to the peaks each night.

The old man said, "I know who you mean, he is my scout. He is away today, but he will soon come home. At any rate, I am the head man here."

So the boy said, "If you are the head man here, I have brought you the prayer offerings the Chief and High Priest and the other head men have made for you."

Well, the old man said that he was very glad that the offerings were made for him, because his people prized them very highly and he took the bundle and opened it and spread the plaques with the pahos on them out in front of him in the middle of the kiva. Then he said to the youth, "Watch me closely and see what I do. Do you see this paho? It was made by a man with a bad heart—I will cast it behind the ladder. But the maker of this paho has a good heart—I will place this in front of the ladder. Now I will call my people and pass these offerings around to them."

So he opened the north, west, south, and east doors of the kiva and as he did this, many people came in and the youth saw that this was a large under-ground dwelling with only one opening through the kiva to the upper world. The youth was surprised to find that, as the head man handed around the pahos, there were certain ones for certain people and that there were just enough for every one.

Finally, the head man asked the youth why his people down there had sent the offerings and what it was they wanted. Well, the boy said that his people wanted to find out who it was that lived up there and if they might be supernatural beings. And they answered him and said that they were the Kachinas, and being Kachinas they had control of the weather, like the rain and the storms.

Now the Kachinas said that they would teach the youth the Kachina dances so that he could show his people down below how to hold Kachina dances and make them a part of their religion.

So the youth was asked to stay for four days and during those four days and four nights he was shown the different dances and he was asked to study them so that he could paint the faces on the ceremonial masks when he returned. So the old man dressed the youth in full costume and they danced to the north, west, south, and east.

Then the youth, who had heard about the Germ God (Muiaingwa) now recognized the old man as the Germ God himself. Then the Germ God told the youth that if he would stay with them for awhile he would teach him how to make masks out of a white material and he told him that he must also learn how to make the costumes and belts and how to prepare the paint. The Germ God said that the youth must also learn their songs and then he said, "This ceremony will surely bring rain if you do as we do up here."

Now after he had learned these dances and memorized the painting and the songs and all that was necessary, he was sent back to his home. Before he left the kiva, he was told that he and his relatives would now be a Kachina Clan. Well, the youth said that they were already the Crow Clan, but the head man said that they had a Crow Kachina and told the boy to tell his uncle, the Chief, that they must make pahos to the Kachinas whenever they held a dance.

When they had told him all this he was sent back. While he was gone his people had been uneasy for four days, for they knew the forest was full of wild animals. When he returned, they were glad.

The youth went to the kiva and the Chief was waiting for him there. The Crier was sent out to call the people to come to the kiva and when the men gathered in the kiva the youth told them how he had been taught the songs and the painting of the masks and how the Kachinas had control of the rain and wished the people to make prayer offerings for them whenever they prayed for rain and held a Kachina dance.

And so the Crow and Kachina Clans brought these dances to the Hopi.

THE LEGEND OF PALOTQUOPI

MANY years ago when the Hopis were living down at Palotquopi they were very progressive and prosperous, on account of having water, and having an irrigating system from the river which flows through that country. There they had taxation by means of doing some donation work on the canals and ditches at certain times of the year. They did not have so many ceremonies then and their most sacred one was Laconti (Basket Dance). In this dance baskets were used, like the ones of Second Mesa today. This ceremony always took place late in the fall and it had always brought them rain and heavy snow up in the mountains. And also their Jejellti (social dances) were not many, the most joyous one was the Butterfly Dance. Being prosperous in their way of living everything was plenty, and why shouldn't they be happy and amuse themselves in some way? So, from one of the kivas, they held a Butterfly Dance with which the spectators were very much pleased. Everybody was talking about it, so the dancers again put it on for two more days, then they thought they would pass it on to the next kiva. So they asked the men of the other kiva to carry on the same dance, and when they had danced, these men passed it on to the next kiva, and so it went around like that until it came back to the kiva from where it was started. In this kind of a dance only the young maidens are supposed to dance, but by this time some of the young married women were taking part and instead of putting it on during the day time in the plaza, they were dancing in the kiva at nights, so they were having a great time of their lives, and it went on from bad to worse. Nobody cared who was whose wife or husband, and finally they got the wife of their chief. In those days the chief or any high priest was not supposed to take part in social dances or was not to be seen in the kiva with the rest of the people. As it was their general rule that they must have patience, and above all must bear in mind peace, and think and pray for prosperity in the years to come, for they knew that the people of any race must have good supplies of food and water to keep their bodies in strong physical condition to defend themselves against an enemy attack. They were good fathers and watched over their people carefully. They were patient and neither heard nor spoke evil. No matter what the people would do or how bad they might be, they were always comforted. But as this dancing went on, it was carried too far and all the rest of the priests had gone crazy except Chief Tawayistiwa, himself. This chief they had, was quite a young man; he had only two small children, and these babies being neglected they would cry at night when they woke up, so the father would take them to the kiva to get the mother to nurse the younger one. When they were quieted down the father would take them back to bed again. On these trips to the kiva at night his wife would sometimes ask him to come down into the kiva and look on while they danced, and of course knowing the law and his duty he always had refused. All these things got so heavy on him that he could bear it no longer, so one evening he went and called on his nephew, Siwiyistiwa, who had grown up to be a good strong young man. While this madness was with the people, men and women of mature age had pleaded with their sons and daughters, telling them of the wrong and crime that they were doing against their father, the chief, and themselves. But it was of no use, it only caused the younger people to lose respect for them, and then the old people were ill-treated, spit upon and fed on the leftovers, which were not very much, for the house duties were neglected by the young women. All this was unbearable for the aged people and for the Chief. So he called at the house of his nephew. He was welcome and seated himself by the fireplace. Siwiyistiwa got up from his seat and handed his uncle a bag of tobacco which hung on the wall near by, and this the uncle smoked. After finishing his smoking, the youth asked him what he had come for.

"Yes," said Tawayistiwa, "after long wanderings in my mind about our children (people) it seems like I am forced to come and have to depend on you to 'sacrifice' yourself, not for the good of any one, but for all—everybody here in my town."

"Yes, you certainly have a lot of patience," said the youth, "to hold out this way, what with all I have seen and know of your wife. I did not want to tell you because I did not wish to be the cause of the weight of your wrath. Because of the sympathy that I have for you I am willing to do what you have come to ask of me."

"I thank you, my nephew," said the Chief. "Thank you. First of all I would like to know if you are strong on your running."

"Yes," said Siwiyistiwa, "I am quite strong."

"All right," said the Chief. "Of course you may be, but I still want you to gain some more strength and speed. So from tomorrow on, you will start to do your running to the foot of the mountain ridge and back. That is quite a distance away, so the best way to time yourself would be by the rising of the sun. For a few mornings the sun will rise before you get back here, but if you are gaining by and by you will get back here away before sunrise, so be sure to get up at the same time in the mornings and be off. I will call again in a few days and will tell you what we will do next."

After the Chief had gone Siwiyistiwa was rather a little worried, but of course, with the Hopi in those days the uncle was over the nephews and nieces. Whenever he asked anything of them it had to be done. While the boy was preparing himself, he didn't know for what, his uncle too was getting things ready for him. The youth was gaining strength and speed and was very light on his feet and he was getting back to the village away before the sun would come up over the horizon. Then Tawayistiwa again went to see his nephew and when he got there he found the youth was waiting for him.

"Come right in and have a seat," said his nephew, getting up and handing him a bag of tobacco as usual. After smoking a pipe he said to the boy, "Again I am here, hoping to find you with more strength and speed."

"Yes," said his nephew, "I have gained some."

"Very well," said his uncle, "I have everything ready for you, so tonight you can come over to my house and there I will tell what to do. But be sure to come after everybody goes to the kiva."

Late that night Siwiyistiwa went to his uncle's house. Upon entering, the Chief took him away into the back room. There they sat down and there his uncle smoked his pipe solemnly over the pahos which he had prepared. Then he said, "Here I have these things ready for you and tomorrow morning early you will take these pahos out with you toward the same direction you have been going and up over the mountain ridge. On the other side is an open range. There you will come upon a herd of deer. Look them over carefully, then make your selection of a young buck with a pair of good weapons (horns), but wait for the sun to appear. Now watch very closely and just as it peeps over the horizon run into the herd. It is those weapons that you are going to get for me, so be sure to keep after your selected buck until you run him down, then after cutting off his two front horns you will deliver to him these pahos that I have here made ready for him, and also my message."

The next morning Siwiyistiwa went out to where he was directed and when he got there he went over the mountains and there in the open he saw a herd of deer. He looked them over very carefully while he was waiting for the sun to rise and just as the sun peeped over the horizon he ran into them and how they made the dust fly! But he kept after them along the side of the mountain range so as to keep them away from the rocky hills. The deer kept falling away one by one, until at last his selected buck was left alone. Now finally this deer gave out and lay down. The boy jumped on him quickly and took hold of his horns and turned his head over. But alas, the deer cried, "Mercy me, have a heart," in plain Hopi, which was of course a very astonishing thing to the youth and he held his breath for a moment. Then he said to the deer, "I am not going to hurt you, I am not going to kill you, I only want your horns, your weapons. My uncle, Tawayistiwa, would like to have them, so he has sent me out here to get them but I don't know why."

"Mercy be upon us!" said the deer. "Has he lost his mind and forgot his 'theory' and law, and is he angry with us all, and will he use my weapons to destroy his town?" Then he sank down in sorrow and in sympathy for all that were ignorant of the coming calamity. Shedding quite a few drops of tears, he then looked up and said, "Take my weapons, but please do not use your knife, because you will hurt me. Just give them a little twist and they will slip off and another pair will grow out again soon."

"Thank you," said the youth as he took off the horns. Then he brought forth his bundle and said to the deer, "Here, I have some pahos which my uncle, Chief Tawayistiwa, has made and sent them to you, hoping to make you all happy. He also said that all you people (game) living down here in the lower country must get to moving and drift over to the higher mountains to the northeast, that you may be saved, so take these pahos to your people and tell them what the Chief has said about moving."

The deer got up and went away with the bundle of pahos which he distributed among his people and told them about the Chief's message, which of course, was a great grief to them all.

The youth went on home taking the two horns which he had taken from the young buck. When he got home Tawayistiwa was waiting for him and as he entered the doorway, "Thanks," said the Chief. "Thanks that you have come already. I did not quite expect you so soon, but you have proved yourself strong and swift. All right, have a seat." As the youth seated himself the Chief got out his bag of tobacco and pipe and then he said to his nephew, "If you have anything that you have brought me you may lay it here before me that I may give it a welcome smoke." So the boy laid the two horns down on a plaque on the floor before the Chief. He was very much gratified with the little horns as though they were for some benefaction of his people. After smoking his pipe, the Chief asked Siwiyistiwa about his trip and the boy told him all about it.

After hearing his nephew's story of his trip, Tawayistiwa said, "You have done well, but there is some more to be done and I have everything ready, so tonight when you come again I will tell you what you will do next."

Late that evening the boy went back to his uncle, and when he got there his uncle was waiting for him. As he entered the house he was welcomed. The Chief was already smoking and the boy seated himself by his uncle. "The weight of all this worry is getting heavier every day as I am preparing these things and I am sad to think that here I am working only for the punishment of my children (people) but this will be the only way out of the trouble and it is necessary to sacrifice you." As he said this he could not help but cry. Tawayistiwa had made masks for him, each one different—Kachina, Yaponcha, Masauwu, and one portion was of fat meat. "Tonight you will wear these masks, one upon another, and carry these weapons of the deer, and you will go the same direction where you have been going for your running, up the mountain range where there is some wood. Build your fire there and when you get enough live coals, take one and put it in the mouth of the top mask and blow on it and this will give the look of having eyes of fire and your fire will be seen from the pueblo. Then come running and when you get here, come through the small south alley and run up the ladder to the top floor of this house. Up there you will find corn in metates. Start grinding for a few moments and then go down again and out the same way. If the men in the kiva be brave and big-hearted they will come out and try to catch you.

With these instructions Siwiyistiwa was dressed up in a dreadful and fearful costume and he went out to where he was directed. He built a fire and the people seeing it from the village wondered who or what it was having a big bonfire, and by the reflected firelight the people could see, even at that distance, something standing in the glow.

The fire went down lower and lower and finally it died out. Then they saw a light coming toward the town, coming closer and closer. When it came up they saw that this terrible being had eyes of fire and those who saw him fell with fright in their doorways or wherever they happened to be. He entered through the alley into the plaza and went to the Chief's house, where he ascended to the top floor and could be heard grinding corn. Then down he came and went out again toward the direction he had come from. Now it happened that there was a little boy who was just thought to be an outcast and he was with some other boys who were looking down at the dance from the kiva top. This boy was not at all frightened and saw everything. He called down into the kiva to the dancers and told them that some dreadful ghost had come, but everybody called him a liar and would not believe him.

This boy, whose name was Kochoilaftiyo (Poker Boy) was just a poor boy and was living with his old grandmother. Regardless of what Kochoilaftiyo had told the people in the kiva about the ghost, the dancing went on with full force until morning. But that day, everybody was telling about this terrible ghost and so the young men declared that they could catch the ghost that night.

After dark the young men placed themselves in many hiding places from where they might leap out at the ghost. But when he came, they all fell down with fright and after coming to they ran for their lives. Kochoilaftiyo was watching the dance from the kiva top, wrapped up in his little mouse skin robe and he was not a bit scared. The young men tried for two nights, but alas, the creature was so frightful that he could not be caught.

The next day the little boy told his grandmother about the ghost. "Grandma," Kochoilaftiyo said, "for three nights some frightful ghost has been coming to the village and the young men have tried to catch him but all have failed."

"It is time," said the old lady, "that we get our warning because of what has been going on. This is a warning of punishment or some calamity which will fall upon us all and it will be something that no one can escape."

"Tonight," said the boy, "they will lay for him again and I would like to be with them. If he is caught I would like to see what he is. It must be something more than man who can handle this thing with magic or witchcraft power."

"So go," said the grandmother, "and get me a sumac branch."

Kochoilaftiyo obeyed his grandma and went out after a little branch. When he came back with it the old woman brought out from the back room her materials of feathers and cotton yarns of which she made two prayer plumes and put them on this sumac twig and with her little pipe she smoked her earnest prayer over her offering to the gods. "Take this, my son," she said to the boy, "to the Masauwu shrine and set it therein and pray for the best, but before you leave look around carefully and if you find there Masauwu's digging stick, pick it up and replace it with this one. This is the exact duplicate of it." As she said this she handed him an old digging stick pretty well weathered. Kochoilaftiyo took the stick and the prayer offering to the shrine. There he placed the pahos, looked around carefully, and seeing the stick he picked it up and replaced it with his grandmother's. Then he came back. The grandmother was very thankful for the stick. "This stick of Masauwu's is a wand of power and with it you might be able to knock down that ghost. So, my dear child," said the old woman, "it may be best that you station yourself in the narrow alley through which he comes and goes."

That evening after dark Kochoilaftiyo, instead of going to the kiva top to look on the dance, went into the alley to wait for the ghost. As he was sitting there in the dark someone came and the boy looked and alas, there was Masauwu himself, standing before him and Kochoilaftiyo was stunned with fright for a moment and could not speak. "You certainly did a wise thing," said Masauwu to the boy, "by taking my stick, but here is something that will hide you and keep you from being seen," and he handed him four grass brush bristles and advised him what to do. Kochoilaftiyo was very thankful and he sat down with the bristles in one hand, the stick in the other, and waited for his chance on the ghost. Now; some of the strong young men had also stationed themselves outside the village to await the coming of the ghost. At the same time, the dancing was still going on in the kiva. Toward midnight the ghost was seen coming and all the supposed brave-hearted fell down with fright, but Kochoilaftiyo was still himself. When the ghost passed him he got up and waited for his return and got ready for the attack. The ghost jumped off the house, ran into the alley, and with all his might Kochoilaftiyo struck him with Masauwu's stick and knocked him down. As he fell, the boy was on top of him and he held his breath for he was half scared then.

Finally he asked, "Who are you?"

"It is I," said the ghost, "but don't ask me more, but take me into the kiva. In there you will see who I am."

As they walked over to the kiva the dancing was on with full force, and when they got on top Kochoilaftiyo called in and he was not heard on account of the beating of the drum and again he called at the very top of his voice. This time he was heard, so he said, "Be courteous to this guest who is my companion for I am not alone." Hearing Kochoilaftiyo's voice, the whole kiva became silent and all held their breath. Finally a voice called out, "Come in. Come right in."

The ghost started down the ladder first with Kochoilaftiyo following him, and the people in the kiva were all looking up to see what was coming in. When the ghost exposed himself to the firelight the people were stricken with fright and fell to the floor. One by one, when they came to, they crawled out of the kiva. Only a few old men were left and the ghost and Kochoilaftiyo seated themselves in front of the firelight. Seeing this frightful creature the old men hung their heads and were silent.

Finally, one of them spoke and said, "For all our conduct of crime it is already too late and we must suffer and who knows what will become of us. Perhaps we may learn from this man, whoever he is, but we can do nothing. Call our father, the Chief," and at this request Kochoilaftiyo went out and called the Chief. He pretended to be very much surprised at being called away in the night, but he took his bag of tobacco and his pipe and went to the kiva with the boy. Coming, he seated himself on the left side of Kochoilaftiyo and before anyone else, he lit his pipe of tobacco and started smoking. Having taken four puffs of smoke out of his pipe he passed it on to the rest of the old men. The pipe went around and was finished up, and then the chief spoke and said, "My dear fellowmen, I wondered why I was called at this time of the night, but I see that you have someone with you."

"Yes," said one of the old men, "this ghost has been coming for the last three nights and this being his fourth night he is caught. He has been going up to your house to the top floor. Therefore, perhaps you might explain to us the meaning of all this. Though we know that we have done wrong against you, we are wondering now if this might not mean more than just to stop this dancing, and worry is upon us now."

"Of all this I do not know," said the chief, "and also the meaning of it I cannot explain. So without any further questions take the masks off the man that we may see who he is." Kochoilaftiyo was asked to take the masks off and as he came to the piece of fat meat the Chief said to put it aside as it is food that the men in the kiva may cook and eat. As the last mask was taken off they saw that he was the Chief's nephew,

Siwiyistiwa, his only nephew, and alas he hung his head and wept.

"Being your own nephew," said the kiva chief (Kiva mongwi), "take him and do what you want with him."

"No," said the Chief, "him I deliver unto you."

Said the kiva chief, "You being our chief, we cannot do otherwise from your wishes, so we demand your advice."

"If you do," said the Chief, "I advise you to bury him alive in the plaza in front of the shrine, with all his masks, before the day comes. But be sure and make a good job of it that he may not escape."

At this command Kochoilaftiyo went out and dug a hole deep enough that Siwiyistiwa's head would be covered under ground when he was sitting down. When he had done this he went back to the kiva and brought Siwiyistiwa out to the plaza and buried him, but before he had him all covered up Siwiyistiwa asked him to come there for four mornings and to take a look for signs of the approaching disaster.

That night the whole town was weary and the old men and women of good mind were stricken with fear. The next morning Kochoilaftiyo went to look at the grave, and behold, there was Siwiyistiwa's hand sticking up out of the grave with four fingers open, which meant that something would happen in four days. The second morning he went again and saw that there were three fingers up and one finger down or closed. Now every morning one more finger would be closed down, until on the fourth morning all the fingers had been closed and his whole hand had disappeared under the ground. The day was gloomy. Clouds were gathering in the skies overhead and around the grave the earth was all wet and boggy. Toward noon it began to rain, coming down heavier and heavier, and then out of the grave a great water serpent of enormous size appeared and stood swaying back and forth and also, at every corner of the plaza others appeared but they were not quite of the size of the one at the shrine, who had come up out of the grave. Now water came shooting up out of the corners of the plaza where these serpents stood swaying, and soon there was water everywhere. The rain kept up and the waters were raising higher and higher. Now the people began to move to the higher ground, taking what they could in the way of food and bedding, and there was much suffering and fear, and all this continued for four days. The only thing they could do was to look at their village standing in the midst of the water, where the great serpent was still swaying back and forth. Of course, the people were in great trouble and hated to leave their homes but still this serpent was so fearful and they wondered if it ever would go away. With weary thoughts of sadness the men set to work making their prayer offerings of many pahos, and when this was done the Chief asked of the people who would be willing to sacrifice their children, because they must make all this offering to the

Great Serpent and ask him to make peace. Now who would part with beloved children? There was a great hesitation among the people, but being the request of the Chief a boy and a girl of six years of age were chosen who were, of course, of clean hearts and innocent. These two were given a tray of pahos and told to walk out into the water toward the great serpent while the people watched with sadness and tears in their eyes. When they had reached this monster he sprang up and coiled himself around the two children and sank with them into the water, which was of course a very terrible sight to the people watching from the hills.

Now everybody was very much discouraged, and though they hated to leave their homes and property they finally gave up all hope and decided to leave the country, but before starting they called a council to select their new chief or leader, because at this time the Chief considered himself guilty of the disaster and no longer worthy to lead his people and the people too felt the same way, but because of the wrong they had done no one dared to say anything. So finally the Chief himself asked the boy, Kochoilaftiyo, to be the chief and as he had been just an outcast, but had done a brave act, he was now looked upon as more than just a human being, on account of his wise Spider grandmother.

"I pray you," said Kochoilaftiyo, "I am not worthy to lead you. I am only a Kocholabi (fire poker) and do not consider myself good enough to take your authority, to be your chief and leader."

"It is not who you are, or what you are that I am considering. It is because of your innocence and the simplicity of your heart that I wish you to be our chief from now on."

"Well," said Kochoilaftiyo, "will you and the people ever forsake me?"

"No," said the Chief, "your wishes and footsteps will be our path and here with my tiponi you shall lead our people."

"I shall not take yours," said Kochoilaftiyo, "I and my grandmother have our own in which we believe and trust and it is without stains of evil. Therefore, we shall take no other in its place. So you shall keep yours. Your kind request and offer of your highness and royalty unto us, we shall not accept, because we will always be looked upon as who we are and what we are and always will be considered as such and no other but that. Why not ask your brother, Tawahongva? I think it is best that your clan should keep this royalty and continue as our chiefs and leaders. As it is today, on this very day we all feel guilty and not worthy to be your children (people) so it is for you and your clan to consider whether you will have mercy and forgive us. We are willing to follow you again. Therefore, I, Kochoilaftiyo, demand for the people that this man, Tawahongva, your brother, be our chief and leader from this day on, as we feel that it is not right for any other clan to take the royalty away from your clan."

"Very well," said Tawayistiwa, "I think you for your great and earnest consideration for my clan, and so your demand for Tawahongva, my brother, to be our chief, is fulfilled." After these last words, Tawayistiwa picked up his tiponi and handing it to his brother, Tawahongva, declared him chief and leader of the people.

When this was done, the people were somewhat relieved of their weariness. Tawahongva set to work and made his pahos or prayer plumes. With these and his sacred corn meal he drew his line or path over which the people were to journey toward the northeastward.

Now, with all this worry and grief two parents had forgotten their children, a brother and sister. These two little children had been sleeping and wakened up while the water was still high. They cried for their mother and father and not only that they were hungry too. So they got up and searched about for something to eat, and finally they found some piki which they ate. By this time the water had gone down a good deal so the two children came down off their house and went around into the plaza and alas! there they saw the great serpent swaying back and forth and they were very much frightened. They stood still for awhile, looking at the monster in great fear, and then suddenly the serpent spoke to them, saying, "Come, be not afraid, I am not going to hurt you. It is sad to see that you two children have been left behind, so be not afraid and come." The serpent was being very sympathetic in asking the children to come, so finally they came up to him. "Please, don't be afraid of me. I am Siwiyistiwa and I am not going to hurt you. I called you here to me to tell you where your parents and the rest of the people have gone. They left here many, many days ago, going toward the northeast, heading for a place called Situqui (Flower Butte) and it is best for you to follow them. You cannot live here because very soon there will not be anything more to eat. If you ever catch up with your people it is likely that you will not recognize your father and mother, so I will tell you their names. Your father's name is Koyoungnu, and your mother's is Sackmunima, and they too will not recognize you and they will ask you your names, so young man, you are Tiwahongva and you, his sister, you are Tawiayisnima, so above all remember your parents' names and your own. Now, you go up over there to the northeast corner house of this plaza and climb the ladders to the very top floor. Up in there you will find some big birds sitting upon the shelves. You must bring them out and let them fly toward the same direction that your people have gone. The feathers of those birds will be used for making pahos of all kinds by your people."

The two children went up to the house as they were directed, and to their surprise they found some odd looking birds with no feathers on their heads, and the ends of their tail feathers were still covered with the foam from the water which had turned them white, and away over in one corner there sat still another bird looking somewhat the same as the others, but the ends of his tail feathers were not white. After letting these birds down from their roosts they spoke to the children, saying, "We all thank you, Tiwahongva and Tawiayisnima, for we are the innocent elderly people. We could not swim and so here we had turned into birds and we are now the turkeys, and from now on our feathers will be helpful to your people for making prayer offerings to the gods."

"And I am the buzzard," said the other strange bird, and with my feathers, after all the sacred ceremonies the members will be 'discharmed' and they will also be used for 'discharming' the sick and evil among all the people. And again we all thank you for letting us down and out, so here we go, and good-bye." As they flew away the buzzard went up and circled around overhead four times to "discharm" the ruined town, then he followed the rest of the birds away toward the northeast. After the birds were gone Tiwahongva and his sister went back to Siwiyistiwa, the serpent, for some more instructions.

"Now," he said to them, "you go up to the west corner and up at the very top floor you will find some sweet corn meal and some piki and also a small robe and gourd to carry your water in. Bundle all that up in the little robe and come back here to me." So they went up there and got what was there.

When they came back again, the serpent said to them, "Now you are ready to go and if you catch up with your people tell them that I, Siwiyistiwa, am now a supernatural being and have power and will do anything for the people in the way of prosperity—I can send them rain and in fact, anything like that will be yours for the asking, so tell them to make pahos for me and set them out anywhere toward this direction, but remember, they must call me by name at the very top of their voices that I may hear and know. Now, like this, 'Siwiyistiwa, here I have made pahos for you. We know and remember your message of promise which was sent to us by Tiwahongva and Tawiayisnima, so please fulfill now your promise of sending us rain for the benefit of our crops and the people, and so forth.' Then the pahos and the message will always be received. Now, I warn you not to look back till you get away over on the other side of the hill. If you do, something might happen to you, so be sure to remember not to look back. Farewell. Take good care of your sister." Tiwahongva and his sister than started out on their long journey and they didn't know where they were going but they were traveling on their way. Being so young, it was hard for them to travel, especially for the little sister, so Tiwahongva would carry her on his back awhile and then let her down again and they would go on like that all day. It was still daylight in the evening when they decided to make camp and were just about opening their bundle of lunch when they heard a loud roaring noise overhead and they were very much frightened and wondered what it could be. Tiwahongva held his sister tightly to his breast, and behold, someone had descended from the heavens all clothed in a glittering costume of ice that sparkled like silver and his head and face shone like a star. He spoke to them and said, "Do not fear, I am So-tukeu-nangwi, the heavenly God and because of the sympathy I have for you I have come to help you, so come get on this shield (Yo-vota) of mine and let us be on the way." When they had climbed onto the shield, up they went into the heavens. The two children had their eyes closed all the way up, until they got there and when they opened their eyes they could see for many miles and everything was grand.

"Now," said So-tukeu-nangwi, "I know you are tired and hungry, so you may now eat," and he cut up a nice ripe muskmelon and set it before them and they ate very delightedly.

When the darkness had covered the earth again this God said to them, "Look to the far north and you will see firelight. There is where your people are now. It does not look so very far away, but that is many, many days journey and you are too young and do not know that this is a big undertaking for you. For this reason, I went to get you and brought you up here, because I know you are too young, but you must understand me and I know you will. I am the wisdom and knowledge and above all else you must have faith in me—faith and trust, honesty and truth. Without faith you shall know nothing. If you have faith your prayers for your people will always be answered, and from now on my teachings will come to you in dreams and there will be more and more as you grow older."

The next morning So-tukeu-nangwi had made everything ready for them to take along upon their journey—seeds of all kinds for the coming season. Said he, "When the spring comes, the warm weather, these seeds you will broadcast outside around the village and they will grow and bear fruit that everybody may eat and they may save the seeds for their own use. Be like the others, play like the other children, but always together. When you catch up and get to your people they will not know you. They have already given you up and have forgotten all about you. Look carefully among them. Your father has a mole under his eye on the right side of his face and your mother has a bunch of gray hair in front on the left side of her head. By these marks you will recognize your own father and mother and you will run to them. These seeds and other things which I have placed in this bundle of your robe must never be handled by anyone, especially this little 'tiponi' (emblem) which needs your particular care. It is this 'tiponi' that you will always set up when you perform my ceremony for the benefit of your people. Now let us be on the way. I will take you close up to your people, that you may camp just for one night, then in the morning after all the meal is over you will be there. They have got their town built now, so you will go straight into the plaza."

The two children had a grand ride on Yovota (shield) and were landed just about a quarter of a day's trip from the town. So-tukeu-nangwi then said, "Farewell" to them and went back up into the heavens.

The next day Tiwahongva and his sister walked into the plaza of the new town. There they stopped and the people stared at them and wondered who they were and where they had come from, so they notified the crier to call out and let the people know, so that they would come to the plaza to see that somebody had come. When the people came, they surrounded them.

Then Chief Tawahongva came forward with a heavy heart of sympathy, "Now, you my people," he said, "is there anyone here that remembers or could recognize these children and tell us who they are and whom they belong to? Is there any parent here that had forgotten or had given them up as dead at the time of the flood, back down at Palotquopi. They must belong to somebody. Who shall claim them? If nobody will, I will now leave it up to them and see if they, themselves, remember and can recognize their own father and mother. Now look carefully among us and see if you know anyone or remember anybody." So the brother and sister looked for the mole on the faces of the men and for the gray hair on the women, by which they were to detect their parents, and all at once they recognized them and with tears in their eyes they ran up to their parents, saying, "You are my father and you are my mother. We are your son and daughter. My name is Tiwahongva and mine is Tawiayisnima."

"My dear children!" cried their parents with tears and they caught hold of them and held them close to their breasts, which of course struck the hearts of all the people and the whole town cried for joy. They were taken to the home of their parents with their little bundle of sacred things and of this they warned them that they must never touch it or open it. To be sure of safe keeping they took it away into the back room and hung it up in the corner.

Thereafter they lived very happily with their parents and the rest of the people. Day after day the wisdom and knowledge was coming to them clearer and clearer so that when the spring came and the days got warmer they did everything that So-tukeu-nangwi had told them to do. They broadcast the seeds and on them it rained and rained. Then the sun came out and shown brightly on them and heated them and caused them to germinate, and in a few days the little plants sprang up. While these

Nasiwum (brother and sister) would play around with the rest of the children they were always telling them not to pull up the plants for they would bear fruit for the people. And every few days it would rain, which kept the plants growing quite fast and all about the town it was all green. Soon the people were noticing the blossoms beginning to bloom on these plants of many kinds and having all these fruitful plants around them they were very happy and when these were ripe and mature everything was plentiful and the people gathered them all in. They lived there happily for a number of years but as they were really heading for Situqui they decided to move on, and so again they were on the long journey and ahead of them they would always send their scouts—men who were good runners and whose duty it was to look for new sites. On their travels they were protected because So-tukeu-nangwi was with them. This time their new location was at Nuvaquayotaka (Chavez Pass—a butte with snow belt on). Here again they lived very prosperously. But knowing that this was not to be their destination they moved on up to Homolovi (east bank of the Little Colorado river, near Winslow). There they were divided into many groups and established their villages here and there.

Their life here was miserable on account of many mosquitos. These insects caused deaths, especially to the young children, so they moved on still looking for Situqui, going through the country that is called the Moqui Buttes, on to Paquaichomo (Water Dust Hill) which is within a few miles of the present Hopi towns, around the First and Second Mesa district. Southeast of them was Awatovi, which was a good sized town but was now in ruins. From this place, Paquaichomo, they sent the scouts back to find the rest of the people who also had left the Homolovi district. It was thought that they might have gone in other directions and sure enough they were found in many different places in small groups. These scouts were sent back to tell them that the Chief and his group were now in sight of Situqui (Walpi), so Chief Tawahongva was calling all his people together. Finally, most of them came on but some of them had already gone to Sioki (Zuni). Tawahongva then sent his messengers to the chiefs of all the different towns asking for permission to be admitted into their villages and to become a part of their people. So to each town a message went, to Walpi, Mishongnovi, Shung-opovi and Awatovi. When the messengers came back with. the news none of the replies were satisfactory and they all felt sad and realized that they were in a very difficult position, being as they were in somebody else's territory. The only thing to do now was to divide themselves equally into groups and go to these towns and try to enter, so then each group had to select their leader or spokesman. In each group was an equal number of each clan, as the Corn, Cloud, Tobacco, Eagle, Sun-forehead, Sand and

Bamboo clans. With the group which went to Shung-opovi, Nasiwum (brother and sister Tiwahongva and Tawiayisnima) and also Kochoilaftiyo and his grandmother went. Each group was now hoping for the best, so they camped within a short distance of these towns and then asked for mercy and to be permitted to enter in and become their people, but the answers from the chiefs were of no satisfaction. Four being the limit of time to do anything or to ask for anything, these people were very much troubled and discouraged on the third day of their request at all these places. The chief at Shung-opovi did not know that he was discarding the best of these groups who were coming to his people, the two Nasiwum who had the wisdom and knowledge of So-tukeu-nangwi and also Ko-choi-laftiyo and his wise old grandmother. Here at Shung-opovi each clan was admitted in, one after another, the Sun-forehead clan was the last to enter. On this last day Nasiwum were more than discouraged—they had given up all hope, and said that they would stay just where they were and they refused to enter into the town. But Kochoilaftiyo and his grandmother went in with the rest. In a few days Nasiwum had disappeared and no one knew where they had gone. At Mishongnovi and over at Awatovi these people had less trouble of being permitted to enter. But at Walpi they had received the same kind of treatment, or even worse than at Shung-opovi, so it was hopeless to try again and they decided to move on to Siotuka (Onion Point).

By this time, old man Masauwu got anxious and excited, so he rushed up to the town to see the people who had taken his name for their clan. He told them that these people whom the chief of Walpi had refused were religious and were honest in their ceremony and that it would bring rain. Said he, "You must not forget and must remember that I am the one that owns this whole territory. The chief here has no more right than just of his town. I am the man that has all the right to say what I think, so hereafter, whoever comes shall enter and stay. With compassionate feelings in my heart I ask for two of your good runners to rush down there and head them off. They are leaving right now."

When these two runners reached them at Tawapa (Sun Spring) their scouts had already gone ahead. Tawahongva and his people had destroy all the crops of the Walpi's because their people had received such disagreeable treatment from the chief. While all this was going on, it was clouding up very heavily overhead and the people had divided themselves—all the women folk on one side and the men on the other. The women had formed in a circle and were singing and dancing the Basket Dance and while this was going on the storm clouds had gathered so heavily that the day was growing very dark and cold and then it started snowing and it kept coming on heavier and heavier. All through the storm and the dancing the two Masauwu clansmen had pleaded earnestly with Tawahongva and his people, telling them that this chief who had refused them was only a sub-chief under Masauwu.

"To make you understand," said the two men, "we are telling you all, Masauwu has all the right here and it is his earnest message of sympathy that we have brought to ask you to come and live with us. We trust and worship him. What the chief has done unto you by this he has only hurt himself and lost his self respect. So trust that we, with all our hearts, are telling you the truth and asking you all earnestly to come with us."

"Well," said Tawahongva, "will it be that you will consider and respect us as you do yourselves as a people? Otherwise we will not turn back to go with you. My scouts have already gone."

"We honestly and truly say that you will have the same right as we have, so over what land your scouts have trotted, this is given unto you. It is yours forever."

During all these pleadings the dancing by the women was kept up and the snow by this time had fallen over a foot deep. At last Tawahongva consented for all his people to return to Walpi or Situqui and all at once the snowstorm turned into rain—a real cloudburst which washed away the snow in a very short while and now the waters were rushing down off the hillsides from the Walpi Mesa. All this water had drained down into the flats and that made nice fertile farming land for the people. Now from that day on to this day, the descendants, generation after generation, of these people from Palotquopi have been living here at these different Hopi villages. But Situqui is no more. This Situqui was where the present Walpi is now situated. There used to be a big sand dune covering this whole mesa and the butte that you see there today was covered, heaped up with sand, and every summer it would be covered with flowers of many different varieties. Later all this sand was drifted away off this mesa, by strong winds, and these sand dunes are now away over above Wepo Spring and are still slowly drifting on.

YAPONCHA, THE WIND GOD

ANY years ago the Hopi were very much troubled by the wind. It blew and blew all the time. The sand drifted away from their fields, and they tried to plant their crops but the wind would sweep the soil away before the seeds would even start to germinate. Sadness and worry were upon everybody and they made prayer offerings of many pahos but there were no results.

Many councils were held by the old men in the kivas, where they smoked their pipes earnestly and asked one another why it was that their gods should turn such strong wind upon them. And after awhile, they decided that they would ask the "little fellows" (the two little War Gods Po-okonghoya and Palongahoya, his younger brother) to help them. Now these "little fellows" were called in. When they came in they wanted to know why they were called. The Hopis said that they needed their help, something must be done to the wind. The "little fellows" said yes, they would see what they could do to help the people.

They told the men to stay in the kiva and make many pahos. Then the "little fellows" went to their wise old grandmother, the Spider Woman, and they asked her to make some sweet corn meal mush for them to take along on a journey. Of course they knew who Yaponcha (the Wind God) was and where he lived—over near the Sunset Mountain in the big cracks in the black rock.

When the corn meal mush was made they came back to the kiva and found the pahos were ready and also the ball which they always liked to take along to play with wherever they went, and the bows and arrows had been made for them, because it was much like going on the warpath for them. So the arrows were of bluebird feathers which were considered most powerful in those days.

The two "little fellows" set out toward the San Francisco Peaks. The old men went with them as far as the Little Colorado River and there they sat down and smoked their pipes.

The little warriors went on and on, playing with their ball. They reached the home of the Wind God, Yaponcha, on the fourth day. The Wind God lived at the foot of Sunset Crater in a great crack in the black rock, through which he is ever breathing and does so to this day. They threw the pahos into the crack and hurriedly took out their old grandmother's sticky cornmeal mush, and they sealed up Yaponcha's door with it. Now he was awfully angry, and he blew and blew, but he could not get out. The "little fellows" laughed and they went home, very pleased with themselves, indeed.

But bye and bye, the people in the villages began to feel that it was very hot. It was getting warmer and warmer every day. Down in the kivas it was so awfully hot that the men came out and the people came from their houses and they stood upon the housetops and looked and looked toward the San Francisco Peaks, to see if there were any clouds coming. But there wasn't even the tiniest bit of a cloud to give a pleasant shadow, and not a breath of air, and the people thought that they would smother.

They thought they must do something right away, so the men made some more pahos and called the "little fellows" again and they begged them to go back to Yaponchaki (House of Yaponcha) right away and tell him that there must be peace, and then give him the pahos and let him out, because this heat was much worse even, than the wind. So the "little fellows" said that they would go and see what could be done to make things better.

On the fourth day they arrived at the house of Yaponcha and they talked together and decided that the best thing to do would be to let Yaponcha have just a little hole open, just enough to let him breathe through, but not large enough for him to come out through, altogether. So they took out some of the cornmeal mush and right away a nice cool wind came out, and a little white cloud appeared and went over across the desert toward the Hopi towns.

When the "little fellows" got home again to the villages, everybody was pleased and they have been very grateful ever since. Ever since that time the winds have been just right, and just enough to keep the people cool without blowing everything away.

Ever since then prayer offerings of pahos, to this day, are made to the Wind God, Yaponcha, in the windy month of March by the chiefs and high priests of the three villages of the Second Mesa.

THE KANA-A KACHINAS OF SUNSET CRATER

AT old Mishongnovi the people lived and at the San Francisco Peaks the Kachinas were living. Over in the old town of Mishongnovi there was a young maiden who would not give up to any young man. Her parents were getting old and the father was not able to do as much work as he used to, so he wished that his daughter would get married. But she had refused all proposals from the young men in her town and also from all the towns around. The old man, her father, was very much discouraged to think of all these young men who had tried their chances with the maiden and had met with failure.

Sometime after this, at the San Francisco Peaks, a young Kachina man heard about this. So he thought he would go over to Mishongnovi and propose to the maiden. When evening came he started out across the desert over to the Hopi towns, but being unknown in the town, he was very much in doubt of what the outcome of his undertaking would be. When he did get there some time early in the night, he found the maiden grinding corn up in the second floor of her house. He went in and stood around for awhile and finally sat down. Then he asked her to stop for a moment and listen, because he would like to speak to her. But she would not stop and just kept on grinding. But finally, after awhile, she did stop grinding.

"Why did you stop?" asked the youth.

"You asked me to stop," said the maiden. "Where are you from?"

"I am from the west," he said, and at this, she thought that he was from Shung-opovi. She saw that he was a very handsome looking young man.

Now the parents, in the room below, had noticed that their daughter had stopped her grinding and they wondered, for they thought that something unusual must be happening up there, but they dared not go up to see what or who it was who had come to see the maiden. Now the girl thought that it was getting late, so she asked the young man to go on to bed and as the boy was going out through the door, she asked him to come back and see her again. She herself now came downstairs to bed and the parents asked her who the young man was. She said she did not know him, though she had asked him to come back again to see her.

Now the very next night the youth went back to see the maiden again and found her grinding corn the same as usual. The parents heard someone go up the ladder and walk over the roof to where their daughter was grinding. She stopped her work and then they thought that it must be the same young man who was there the night before. They hoped that the maiden might be interested in this handsome youth and indeed he did interest the maiden. So she asked him again, "Where is your home?" And he said as before, "Over in the west," and again she thought that he meant that he lived in Shung-opovi.

Now the maiden liked this handsome youth very much indeed. She said, "In four days I will go back with you. I will be prepared by that time So come back upon that day and take me to your home."

When the fourth day came, she prepared herself and had her hair done up in butterfly wings (poli-ia-na) and got ready some corn meal and some piki, which she must take with her on her journey. When the boy came everything was ready and he took the tray of corn meal while she carried her piki. They started out and when they got outside of the village the youth said, "Wait awhile, I will see if we can travel easier and faster than we could walk, for we have some distance to go."

He then reached into a little pouch which he was carrying and pulled forth something and threw it from him, westward, across the country, and the maiden saw it was a rainbow like a path before them and she was very afraid. But she had already started out with him and she could not turn back.

"Now let us get on," said the youth, and when they stepped upon it, the rainbow drew itself up to the other end and when they landed they found that they were close to the Little Colorado River. From there again the youth threw his magic in the same direction. The rainbow appeared and they mounted it again and this time they landed on the south side of Palotsmo, Sunset Crater, or the home of the Kana-a Kachina. Here there was a little cloud hiding itself among the pine trees and he was a Kana-a Kachina and he spied the Kachina youth from the San Francisco Peaks taking a Hopi girl with him. The maiden was weary and begged to take a rest and asked the youth to wait a little where he was, for her.

She walked away some distance and presently she heard a voice which seemed to come from under her feet. The voice said, "Be careful, so you may not step on me." And the maiden stopped and looked about her but could not see anyone. It was the Spider Woman who spoke to her, and as the maiden moved to one side, she saw the light down in a little kiva where the good Spider Grandmother lived. She asked the maiden to come in and when she entered the Grandmother said to her in deep sympathy, "My dear child, I have to tell you because you do not know, being only a child. Down in my heart I sympathize with you very deeply. You are out on your first trip and it may be your last trip, and you may not ever see your father and mother again. We cannot hesitate very long. Now I am going with you and I am prepared to go. If we win or lose I am willing to die with you. The youth is a Kachina from San Francisco Peaks and when you reach his home the Kachina people will give you some very difficult tasks to perform, and without my help you would surely fail. Quickly, put me in your ear and let us be on our way." The little Spider Woman was so invisible inside of the Hopi maiden's ear that she could not be detected by anyone, even a Kachina youth.

When the maiden joined the boy again, he threw the rainbow up towards the Peaks and they mounted upon it to take another leap. Now all this time the Little Cloud who was hiding in the pines, knew what was going on, for this little cloud was one of the Kana-a Kachinas who lived in the Sunset Crater. This time the youth and the maiden landed right close to a great kiva far up in the Peaks and they descended from the rainbow and walked up to it.

The youth approached the opening and calling in, he said, "Be courteous to this guest who is my companion, for I am come and am not alone."

And a voice called out from the kiva, "Come in, come right in."

They went in and there they found one old lone man sitting by the fire in the fire-place. The old man begged the young maiden to sit down, and getting up he spread out his own wildcat skin robe for her to sit down upon. Now the whole kiva was very quiet and after she had seated herself she noticed that the youth had disappeared and she did not know where he had gone.

The old man was slowly poking into the fire trying to get more light and he called out saying, "Mother of the House and you, young maiden, come forth. Some stranger has come and she has entered into our kiva."

All this time the Spider Grandmother was whispering her advice into the ear of the Hopi maiden and telling her what she should do.

Now from the north side of the kiva a handsome woman came forth. She seemed suspicious, although she acted with great politeness. The grandmother of the Hopi maiden had already told her of the character of this woman called Hahai-i Wu-uti.

Now the maidens of the house came forth also, and they served her with food and when she was through they cleared it away.

By this time it was quite late in the night, so the old man said, "It is time to go bed," and the handsome Kachina woman, Hahai-i, then opened the door on the north side of the kiva and she asked the maiden to enter and she told her that this was the room where she was to sleep. Now this was the place where the North Wind lived, and as Hahai-i was leaving the room, she said to the maiden, "It is quite cold in here but you will have to do the best you can to get through the night."

Just as soon as the door was closed the Grandmother hastily pulled out some turkey feathers from the bosom of her dress and putting one down on the ground, she asked the girl to lie down on top of it. Then she put one over her, one at her feet, then at her head, and one on either side. And the maiden soon fell asleep, for she was very tired, and the good little Grandmother's turkey feathers kept her warm. Now the wind was blowing very hard all night and it hailed and it snowed and when she woke in the morning she was under a pile of snow. Just as she became awake, Hahai-i opened the door and peeked in, thinking that the maiden had frozen to death. But finding her still alive, she was surprised and asked, "How did you rest ?"

"Very comfortably," said the maiden, and she got up and went out into the kiva room. No sooner had she done this than she was shown to the *mata* (the place for grinding corn) and instead of corn Hahai-i came out with a basketful of icicles and put them into the *mata* for the maiden to grind. The poor maiden felt very cold and unhappy to think she had to grind these icicles and then she thought of her turkey feathers and she took one in each hand with which she would hold *mata-ki* (the mano) so that her hands would not get cold. The icicles were very cold and hard to grind, but she had to go on; she had to grind and grind. The icicles were cold and slick and she could not hold them between the two rocks. Every once in a while Hahai-i would come and take a look to see if she was getting the icicles melted, which she had intended the maiden to do.

Now the Spider Grandmother took a bit of her magic root of an herb and put it in the girl's mouth and asked her to chew it well and then spray it over the icicles. She did this, and no sooner had it touched the icicles than they melted and turned into water in the mata. Now this was the maiden's first test, and when Hahai-i came again and saw what the bride-to-be had done, she was glad. The maiden continued to do this for four days and she spent four nights in the cold room with the North Wind. At the end of four days she finished her test and it was found that she had won over the Kachinas, so she was married to the youth who had brought her there from Mishongnovi. The Grandmother was glad to have been able to serve the Hopi maiden and bring her successfully through her trials. She had put up many jars of water for the Kachinas by grinding the icicles and snow.

Now the maiden's wedding robes and many other presents were brought to her and she was ready to be sent home. Many Kachinas were to go along with her to carry the presents to Mishongnovi, and the bride and bridegroom were dressed in their wedding robes.

This day was rather a joyful day for the bride for she thought of how wonderful the Spider Grandmother had been and how she had helped her to win. And now she was going back home and taking her husband along. And she was very thankful indeed to the little old woman.

On the way back to Mishongnovi at Sunset Crater, the girl stopped just as she had done on the way over and walked away a little to take a rest. But this time, she took her little Grandmother back to her home, and when they got there they both cried for joy. For the last time the girl thanked her again. The Little Cloud who detected the couple on their way up to the San Francisco Peaks was again hiding in the pines and he saw everything that took place.

Now during these four days the parents of the maiden had been very much worried because they did not know where she had gone. So in Mishongnovi this was rather an exciting afternoon for the people to see this girl who had been missing so long coming home with the Kachinas and bringing all kinds of presents. The Kachinas gave all their presents to the villagers and then returned to their home.

From this time on the Hopi were very prosperous for a number of years until finally the men of one kiva, and these were the troublemakers of the village, plotted to see how they could break up the happiness of the Kachina youth and the Hopi maiden and win her love away from her husband. These wicked men made a costume exactly like that which the Kachina man wore and so one day, one of these young men dressed up like him and went to see the Kachina's wife while he was away. On his return he found that his wife cared for someone else, but she herself did not know that it was another man because of the costume and everything being exactly like her husband. So the Kachina man, without making any further trouble, told his wife that he had to go away to his home in the San Francisco Peaks and back to his own people, and so he did. But as he was leaving, he took one of the longest ears of corn from the stack in the house and carried it back with him to the San Francisco Peaks.

Two years later a famine came upon the Hopi people. They prayed and prayed for rain and held ceremonies of many kinds, all of which were of no use. No result came from any of them.

Finally Kana-a Kachinas at Sunset Crater, felt compassion for the people and took mercy upon them. Now they knew that the Mishongnovi maiden had not been treated fairly and they knew of all the hard tests that she had had to go through in the kiva of the San Francisco Mountain Kachinas, and they did not think it right for these Kachina people to bring this terrible calamity upon the whole people. The Kana-a Kachinas then took much sweet corn and strung it up with yucca and many other good foodstuffs. They came across the desert to the Hopi villages to make the people happy and to relieve their hunger. Now when they got there they went dancing through the streets and distributed their sweetcorn and food to the people. But they asked the people not to eat everything up that day which they had received and told them that each family must leave an ear of corn in the corner of their empty storage room.

All the people were made happy and glad so they asked these Kachinas not to go back to their Sunset Crater home, but to live with them always there. But they, being supernatural beings, could not do this, so of their own choice, they went to a little butte which stands by Mishongnovi today, and they opened it up and went in. So that to his day the little butte is called Kana-a Katchin-ki.

Waking up the next morning, to their wonder, the people found that their empty rooms were full of corn and from then on joy was with the people again. After this the Kana-a Kachina dance was celebrated every year until 1902.

THE LADDER DANCE AT OLD SHUNG-OPOVI

The present Hopi pueblo of Shung-opovi has occupied its present site since about 1700. Previous to that time, the pueblo straggled over the foothills at the mesa base. About a hundred yards west of this pueblo, over a sharp ridge, lay the old walled-in spring called Shungopa, the spring that gave the name to the pueblo, and which went dry in the 1870's at the time of a landslide which caused a local earthquake.

About a hundred yards south of this spring stands a large boulder. On the top of this boulder can be observed three holes in a row, each hole being about a foot in diameter and between a foot and two feet deep. Hopi tradition associates these holes with a Hopi ceremony now extinct call the Ladder Dance.

THERE WAS one kiva at old Shung-opovi known as the Ash Pile Kiva. They knew but one dance and that was called the Coal Kachina dance. This kiva was composed of not well-to-do people. Not having many costumes, all they had to wear for kilts were old dresses discarded by the women. The men in the kiva gave the Coal Kachina dance so often that it grew monotonous to see those Coal Kachinas. So one day they made an announcement that they would give another kind of dance in four days. The men in the other kivas said that only some more Coal Kachinas would come into the kiva. About a day after the announcement was made, the boys went out hunting. While they were out, one of the boys got away from the party, and, as he was going around, he jumped a rabbit out of a bush and he chased after it. The rabbit just kept going westward and the boy just kept following it. Well, the rabbit finally got into one of the shrines above Burro Springs, and the rabbit went around back of the shrine and the boy thought the rabbit was all in and tired and ready to lay down. When he got around the shrine he saw a kiva. When he looked in he asked if the rabbit had gone in there. The men who were there said "Yes," and they asked the boy to come in.

When he got in there, they sat him down beside the fireplace and gave him a welcome smoke. When he finished that they told him they had sent the rabbit out to get him and bring him there because they were rather sorry that the men in the other kivas made fun of the Ash Pile Kiva. Then they told him they would like to have two or three of the boys go over to the San Francisco Peaks. There they would show them different kinds of Kachina dances from which they could choose which of the dances they would have in their kiva. So they asked the boy to go right back home and tell the rest of the men of his kiva.

When he came home he went right into the kiva. Well, he told these men what he had seen at the shrine and what news he had been told. He asked the old men to make some prayer offerings which they would take over to the San Francisco Peaks to the main Kachina Kiva and said this must be kept secret from the other people who would be expecting to see the Coal Kachina dance again. They stayed up late to make their prayer offerings so that the boys could start out early for the San Francisco Peaks before the rest of the village woke up. So they came to the foot of the main peaks that day. The next morning about dawn they started to climb and at sunrise reached the kiva. When they got there they were asked to come in, and there they found the same men that the boy saw at the shrine at Burro Springs. So, as usual, they were given their welcome smoke. The men said that they would show them different kinds of dances without losing much time for there was now little time before the dance at Shung-opovi.

So they danced many dances for them and the boys liked the ladder dance very much. Well, the men at the kiva said the dance was difficult because the dancers had to climb a limber young Douglas fir tree. Finally the boys decided to ask these people if they could not do it for them. The people agreed to do the ladder dance themselves because it would be so difficult for the people at Shung-opovi. So when they did agree to do this they sent the boys back, but they asked them to take back home with them two young Douglas firs each about a foot high. They told them that when they got home, they were to find a rock on which to plant these two trees. When they got home with the two firs they brought them into the kiva and the men in the kiva performed a ceremony of welcoming the firs and the boys by smoking.

The next morning the boys took the two trees and went up to the rock which they thought would be best to plant the trees on. That morning the whole village noticed the two trees on top of the rock and wondered what was going to happen. One by one they went to look. There was an old man up there on watch so that no one could hurt the trees. Everyone who went asked him what they were for but he told them not to be too anxious until night came.

That day towards evening the Kachinas began to come out of the kivas. They kind of paraded around the village. At that time the men from the Ash Pile Kiva came out all wrapped up in their blankets. These men went out to meet the real Kachinas who came from the San Francisco Mountains. By that time it was clouding up. These men met the Kachinas at the place called Lonatchi, a spring which lies about a mile west of Old Shung-opovi. When they met them, the Kachinas told the men they must hide out that night so that he people would believe that they were putting on the dance. So they decided they would stay there and the Kachinas would go to the village and the men could follow after dark.

This old man at the rock under the two fir trees would sprinkle cornmeal on the trees and they would grow about an inch or two, and by that time the Kachinas got there they were quite tall trees. In this ceremony each Kachina was in a different costume, except that the two who were to climb the trees were dressed alike. When the people saw the Kachinas on the hill around the rock, they all ran up there. They carefully observed the performance. They were trying to figure out who the Kachinas were. They resembled men in the different kivas. The two Kachinas climbed the trees. The trees were so slender that the Kachinas swayed back and forth. They climbed while the rest sung around. It seemed as if the two trees had a spirit as the two Kachinas swung back and forth. The song that the Kachinas sung, the people of Shung-opovi still sing.

Well, after this performance they went to the village. They paraded around and entered the kiva. Then rain came down. The rest of the kivas felt jealous. Every once in awhile they would send up a man to peep in to see if it were true that the men in this kiva were putting on the dance. About midnight the dance started. All the Kachinas from the other kivas were out. But the men from the other kivas did not dance. They just put away their costumes and followed the new Kachinas around. And then by that time the men who were supposed to put on the dance came in. They watched the dance too and were not recognized.

After the dance was over the Kachinas went back into the kiva. They were supposed to go down the Sipapu and go home that way. So the next day after the dance this kiva was given praise because they had put on a great dance, different from anything that had ever been seen. From that day this kiva was recognized because of this dance, whereas, before they had never been recognized by the people of the village. From then on the people at Shung-opovi held this kind of a dance every four years until the town was abandoned (between 1680 and 1700).

THE LADDER DANCE AT PIVAHONKIAPI

Northwest of Oraibi, seven or eight miles, on that broad terrace which so conspicuously encircles many of the Hopi mesas, about 200 feet below the rim, lie the ruins of two pueblos. The nearest to Oraibi occupies a point which projects from the mesa and is called Hukovi, "The Place of the Winds," or "Windy Point." Two miles farther along the ledge, at the base of a large rock, the pueblo of Pivahonkiapi covers the shelf.

Potsherds tell us that Hukovi and Pivahonkiapi were occupied in the twelve hundreds. We, therefore, assume that the two pueblos were abandoned, like so many others in northern Arizona, because of the great drought of 1275 to 1299 which shows so well in Dr. A. E. Douglass' studies of the tree rings.

About these pueblo ruins, Hopi traditions cluster. At Hukovi the girls were beautiful but bad. At Pivahonkiapi among the gamblers lived a handsome youth. At Achamoli, halfway between Hukovi and Oraibi, lived the two little war gods, sons of the Sun, Po-okonghoya and his brother, Palo-onghoya, with their grandmother, the Spider Woman. What more can you ask as the basis for a story!

About 100 yards east of Pivahonkiapi can be observed eight circular holes, about eight inches in diameter, cut in the rock at the cliff edge. About one of these holes the rock has cracked. The Hopi believe that these holes belong to the "ladder dance."—Ed.

A Pivahonkiapi there dwelt a handsome young man. Two miles away on Windy Point lived two girls in the pueblo of Hukovi. These girls wanted to marry this handsome youth, but he would not look at either of them. This made them mad.

They knew that he was to take the part of a Kachina in a "ladder dance" to be held at Pivahonkiapi in March. The girls thought that this would be a chance to destroy him.

The dance was announced and the dancers practiced the songs in the kiva for eight days. Four days before the ceremony, two youths were selected to go to the San Francisco Peaks which the Hopis call Nuvatekiaovi (The Place of Snow on the Very Top) to get two fir trees, and one of the youths was the handsome young man.

On the way to the peaks they followed a trail and because they were tired they stopped to rest. The handsome youth stepped aside off the trail. Here he met the Spider Woman. She said, "I am in sympathy with you because I know what is going to happen to you. Change your pahos (prayer offerings) as the ones you are carrying are bad. Cast them somewhere and take mine and put them in the shrine. If you don't do that, the witches will surely get you. On your way home, stop and see me."

Returning to the trail he joined his companion and went on to the peaks and placed the pahos in the shrine. There they selected two small fir trees about two feet high.

On his way back the handsome youth remembered to stop and call on the Spider Woman. He left his companion by the trail and hunted up the old woman. The old woman said, "Take the pipe of your father and make smoke so the clouds will hide our path from the witches." So he lit his pipe and she brought him to her kiva. He set down his trees and sat on a skin. "My dear grandchild," said the old woman, "do as I say or your last day will be the day of the ceremony."

She handed him some medicine and said, "The wise men will sing and the tree will grow too fast. Chew this medicine and spit it out on the tree, so the tree may be limber but it will not break." Then she gave him a little light white feather of an eagle and placed it under his heart so that it would make him lighter.

By this time the sky was covered with clouds and he rejoined his companion. He did not say much because he was worried. That night they got home and entered the kiva with their two fir trees. All the men smoked and when they stopped, asked them what they saw in the way of prosperity. They said that they saw good flowing water, so the old men knew that the summer would be good.

While this was going on the old Spider Woman, (she was a great old woman), sent word to the other Spider Women that lived near Pivahonkiapi (she sent the message by way of dreams) to send out her two little war gods, Po-okonghoya and his brother, Palo-onghoya-her grandsons-to look over the place where the tree was to be planted.

As they were small boys no one would notice them as they played with the other children of the village. The boys investigated and discovered that the girls of Hukovi had cracked the rock about the hole in which the tree was to be planted. They hurried back to their grandmother and reported.

"If that is the case," said the old Spider Woman, "I will have to go there and see. I have not got a thing to mend that rock with. One of you boys run and get an ear of baked sweet corn." When the boy had found it, she ground it up as fine as she could. Then she mixed the meal into dough—like the finest clay. When this was ready the day of the ceremony had arrived.

The Kachinas put on their costumes at the mesa foot as they were supposed to come from the San Francisco Peaks. Everyone gathered on the house-tops watching them climb up the mesa. While everyone's attention was so occupied, the old Spider Woman and the boys tried to mend the crack in the rock with the dough. When it was mended, she gave some medicine to the two boys who chewed it up and spat it out on the crack and blew on the crack.

As soon as they had finished, the Kachinas entered the village and marched about the two kivas four times.

In this ceremony, you must know, the leading Kachina, though a man, takes the part of a Kachin-mana (Maiden). In this dance the leader was a notorious wizard who was being paid by the girls of Hukovi to do crooked work.

After making the rounds of the kiva, the Kachinas marched to the place on the edge of the cliff where the trees were to be planted. The Kachin-mana carried the two little trees. When the Mana gave the handsome boy the wrong tree, and the other boy the right tree, he knew the wizard was trying to get him. Both boys laid the trees down on the rock. Someone said something and the leader and everyone looked the other way and the boys exchanged the trees, He knew his tree for it had a feather fastened to one of the leaves.

The trees were now planted in the holes that had been prepared. The Kachinas, standing in a row, started to dance and sing. Slowly the trees began to grow. They grew and grew until they reached 25 to 30 feet high. The two Kachinas that were to climb, one of them being the handsome boy, stood by the trees. Finally the Kachin-mana, the wizard, told them to climb. The young man trusted the old Spider Woman. He chewed the medicine and spat on the tree and climbed slowly. When he reached the top the tree swayed back and forth. All the people on the house-tops thought that the tree would break and he would go over the cliff. He came down and danced and then went up again. When he came down and danced he climbed the tree the third time, swinging back and forth. The girls from Hukovi were on the house-tops with the inhabitants of the village. They wondered why the rock did not give way. When he climbed the fourth time the leader told the youth to climb faster and swing back and forth harder, and swing good and hard with all his might. But still the tree did not break nor the rock crack. When he had climbed down the leader told him to go up a fifth time, but someone had counted so the chief said that was enough as they had gone up the four ceremonial times.

Later the two young men who had climbed the trees took the prayer offerings and started back to the San Francisco Mountains to place them in the shrine. The rest of the Kachinas entered the kiva with the men of the pueblo and all smoked.

Before the men had entered the kiva, the girls from Hukovi hired a wizard to cut the beams in the back part of the kiva. They were mad at the leader of the Kachinas, the Kachin-mana, and the boy. They did not know that he was already on his way to the peaks.

While the smoking ceremony was on, the kiva roof caved in. Everyone was killed but one poor old man far back in one corner who was not a man of high standing but was a common person who never rushed up in front. This old man dug his way out.

The village was in trouble. All the men were killed except the two youths and the old man. Well, of course you know, everyone was sad for many days. The old man knew that everyone was sad so he thought he would do something. So the old man went off by himself and practiced a dance under the cliff. While he was practicing, a girl found him, and he asked her to join him in the dance. She accepted so the old man went to work and made a mask so no one would know her. He took some corn, boiled it well, late one afternoon. He fixed up the girl as well as himself in a Kachina costume. The old man told her to hold out all the nerve she could. When they went to the plaza, the people saw them come. All the people started to cry, but soon got all right. Then the old man and the girl danced and gave out presents of corn.

That night the handsome youth was outside the pueblo where he went every night. He heard something and lay still. He listened. He heard a sound coming closer and closer. It finally came and passed by. It was a ghost dressed in white. He was scared and fainted. After laying insensible for a while, he came to himself. He followed the ghost to the village. When he got to the plaza, the ghost was sitting on the shrine. It was a woman ghost. He went up and asked her why she was there and where she had come from.

She said, "I come from the Colorado River. I come because I sympathize with the people of Pivahonkiapi. I have nothing for you but if you wish to get even with the girls of Hukovi, I would like to help you. I would like to have a prayer plume from everyone in the pueblo and I ask you to have them made this very night. You must keep it a secret why they are to be made."

So the youth went from house to house and every woman made a prayer plume (paho). The boy collected them and gave them to the ghost and said, "We have done what you asked us to do." The ghost took the prayer offerings and thanked him. She said, "I will do everything that you ask me to do. Now what do you want me to do? I can drive them eastward or I can drive them westward. I can even drive them over the cliff." The boy said, "Drive them westward."

Then the ghost went over to Hukovi and she made a noise as if she were dying. She rolled on the ground and moaned. This scared the people. Some boys said they were not scared and offered to kill the old ghost.

The next night the boys lay in wait for her and when she started to moan they got scared and ran away. Everyone got scared. The ghost came back six or seven nights. The people could not sleep for her moaning, so they decided to leave the pueblo.

They packed up their belongings and left the village. The ghost drove them westward. They camped for the night by the Dinnebito, Wash at Bang-wu-wi (Mountain Sheep Cliff). The old ghost came again and kept them awake. But they could not move that night on account of the children.

The next day they moved to near where the Dinnebito Store is and camped. The ghost came early and kept them awake till daylight. Again they started on, and on the third night camped by the Little Colorado River. The ghost came just after sundown because she was near her home and kept them awake till dawn.

At daylight they started on again and camped in the Cinder Hills. Still the ghost came after them. The fifth night they camped by Mormon Mountain. The ghost followed them. On and on they went, crossing the Big Colorado into California. They say that their descendants are now the Mission Indians of California.

DR. FEWKES AND MASAUWU
THE BIRTH OF A LEGEND

In the autumn of 1898, the late Dr. Fewkes, archaeologist of the Smithsonian Institution, was staying at Walpi, one of the Hopi Indian Pueblos. In the annual report of the director of the Bureau of Ethnology his visit is noted as follows:

"In November, Dr. J. Walter Fewkes repaired to Arizona for the purpose of continuing his researches concerning the winter ceremonies of the Hopi Indians, but soon after his arrival an epidemic of smallpox manifested itself in such severity as to completely demoralize the Indians and to prevent them from carrying out their ceremonial plans, and at the same time placed Dr. Fewkes in grave personal danger. It accordingly became necessary to abandon the work for the season."

The Hopis at Walpi have another story of the cause of Dr. Fewkes' departure.—Ed.

ONE OF the most important of the Hopi winter ceremonies is the Wuwuchim which comes in November. At a certain time during the ceremony the One Horned and the Two Horned Societies hold a secret rite in a certain part of the pueblo, and all the people who live on that plaza go away and close their houses. No one may witness this ceremony, for Masauwu, the Earth God, is there with the One Horned Priests who do his bidding in the Underworld and the Spirits of the dead are there and it is said that anyone who sees them will be frozen with fright or paralyzed or become like the dead.

Masauwu owns all the Hopi world, the surface of the earth and the Underworld beneath the earth. He is a mighty and terrible being for he wears upon his head a bald and bloody mask. He is like death and he clothes himself in the raw hides of animals and men cannot bear to look upon his face. The Hopi say he is really a very handsome great man of a dark color with fine long black hair and that he is indeed a great giant. When the Hopi came up from the Underworld and looked about them in fear, the first sign which they saw of any being of human form, was the great footprints of Masauwu. Now Masauwu only walks at night and he carries a flaming torch. Fire is his and he owns the fiery pits. Every night Masauwu takes his torch and he starts out on his rounds, for he walks clear around the edge of the world every night.

Dr. Fewkes had been in the kiva all day taking notes on what he saw going on there. Finally the men told him that he must go away and stay in his house for Masauwu was coming, and that part of the ceremony was very sacred and no outside person was ever allowed to see what was going on. They told him to go into his house and lock the door, and not to try to see anything no matter what happened, or he would be dragged out and he would "freeze" to death. So he went away into his house and he locked the door just as he had been told to do and he sat down and began to write up his notes.

Now suddenly he had a queer feeling, for he felt that there was someone in the room, and he looked up and saw a tall man standing before him, but he could not see his face for the light was not good. He felt very much surprised for he knew that he had locked the door.

He said, "What do you want and how did you get in here?" The man replied, "I have come to entertain you."

Dr. Fewkes said, "Go away, I am busy and I do not wish to be entertained."

And now as he was looking at the man, he suddenly was not there any more. Then a voice said, "Turn your head a moment," and when the Doctor looked again the figure stood before him once more, but this time its head was strange and dreadful to see.

And the Doctor said, "How did you get in?", and the man answered and said, "I go where I please, locked doors cannot keep me out! See, I will show you how I entered," and, as Dr. Fewkes watched, he shrank away and became like a single straw in a Hopi hair whisk and he vanished through the key hole.

Now Dr. Fewkes was very much frightened and as he was thinking what to do, there was the man back again. So he said once more to him, "What do you want?", and the figure answered as before and said, "I have come to entertain you." So the Doctor offered him a cigarette and then a match, but the man laughed and said, "Keep your match, I do not need it," and he held the cigarette before his horrible face and blew a stream of fire from his mouth upon it and lit his cigarette. Then Dr. Fewkes was very much afraid indeed, for now he knew who it was.

Then the being talked and talked to him, and finally the Doctor "gave up to him" and said he would become a Hopi and be like them and believe in Masauwu, and Masauwu cast his spell on him and they both became like little children and all night long they played around together and Masauwu gave the Doctor no rest.

And it was not long after that Dr. Fewkes went away but it was not on account of the smallpox as you now know.

Although Dr. Fewkes never reported this story to the outside world, the Hopis now tell that he related it to the priests in the kiva the next day after the strange occurrence. We can see how in less than forty years a legend had its birth.—Ed.

Made in the USA
San Bernardino, CA
23 November 2015